# HEALTHY COUNTRY COOKING

# HEALTHY COUNTRY COOKING

RUBY M. BROWN

MILNER

HEALTH

SERIES

First published in 2000 by **Sally Milner Publishing Pty Ltd** PO Box 2104 Bowral NSW 2576 AUSTRALIA

Special thanks to Cindy Croker from Barbara's Storehouse in Bowral for allowing us the use of her kitchenware items.

© Ruby M. Brown 2000

**Editing** Lyneve Rappell  **Design** Ken Gilroy  **Photography** Sergio Santos  **Printing in Hong Kong**

National Library of Australia Cataloguing-in-Publication data:

Brown, Ruby M

Healthy country cooking.

Includes index.

ISBN 1 86351 267 5.

1. Cookery. I. Title. (Series: Milner health series).

641.5

**Disclaimer** The information in this instruction book is presented in good faith. However, no warranty is given, nor results guaranteed, nor is freedom from any patent to be inferred. Since we have no control over the use of information contained in this book, the publisher and the author disclaim liability for untoward results.

## Foreword

HEALTHY COUNTRY COOKING represents Ruby's grand collection of traditional country cooking favourites 'with a twist'. Recipes modified, where required, (shown in a second colour) to reflect the current interest in 'lighter' eating for better overall health.

These recipes have been reduced in fat, salt and sugar where necessary; and boosted with fibre where possible. In the interest of heart health, the type of margarine and oils used in the recipes are monounsaturated plant oils rather than the 'heavier' animal fats like butter, dripping and cream.

Most importantly, the flavour and result of Ruby's products have kept their traditional quality, while being better for our bodies.

*Healthy Country Cooking* is a showcase of Ruby's natural flair for cooking and her interest in maintaining good health. She teaches cooking modification skills as part of 10-week health and weight control programs at a local Community Health Centre. Always impressing the participants with unique and interesting ways to 'play' with recipes – for a healthier result.

Ruby M. Brown is a multi-talented culinary author and food technology educator. Her niche, as an author, is in the area of special diets, where she has published a variety of books including Good Food for Diabetes, Wheat Free Cooking and Milk Free Cooking. Student textbooks and a craft book, *Decorated Eggs*, add to Ruby's impressive range of successful writing.

Ruby's delightful manner glows through this book. It is interestingly illustrated and provides a stimulating insight into the lives of yesteryear. The result is a fresh-to-read book to suit the kitchen and the coffee table.

Judy Wellins

B.Sc (Nutr.) M.Sc. (Nutr. & Diet.)
Accredited Practising Dietitian

## Acknowledgments

I wish to express my most sincere thanks and appreciation to my family and others who have made many contributions to the publication of this book.

To my precious husband Kevin – for all the time, love and understanding expressed in our home while this book was being written. Without his untiring support for my work as an author, this book would never have been possible.

To my daughters who now have their own homes – it is lovely to see their love for preparing food, which they first developed in our country home.

To Jan Granger – for her help with proofreading.

To Emily Calvert – how blessed I am to have her work with me in my Country Kitchen.

To Judy Wellins – for her expertise as a nutritionist.

To Maria Manton – for her advice as a dietitian.

To Rosemary Stanton – for her continued interest in my work. She has always been my mentor and I thank her.

To Libby Renney and the staff of Sally Milner Publishing – it has always been a pleasure to work with a group of such wonderful people.

To those people to whom I gave my firm word that I had finished my writing career – please don't 'badger' me about another book, just enjoy this one!

Lemon Meringue Pie (see recipe page 73)

## Introduction

Many things have changed since I first started writing over 20 years ago. We have gone through phases of 'low-cholesterol', 'low-fat', 'low-salt' and 'high-fibre' cooking. Each phase has contributed to healthier eating. Facts and fads come and go as the years go by. However, the basic principles of dietary health remain unchanged. A wide variety of good wholesome food – which also looks good and tastes good – should be foremost in our daily food choices.

People have always wanted traditional recipes like Bread and Butter Custard (page 64).

This book presents favourite country recipes that will delight your palate, with options for making them suitable for a healthier eating program. For instance, butter produces a rich, full flavour in a recipe like Shortbread (page 109). Many of us, however, aim to reduce our total fat intake and may choose to use mono-unsaturated margarine. So, included with each recipe are healthier measurements, ingredients and procedures, offering reduced fat, sugar and salt, and high fibre alternatives.

The message I would like to bring is to follow a healthy diet that provides balance, moderation and variety.

## Healthy Choices

### Making Choices
Life is all about making choices.

When it comes to food choices, there is a lot to consider. The Australian Guide to Healthy Eating* promotes enjoying a variety of nutritious foods every day, emphasising the positive aspects of eating. Foods should be eaten from each food group every day, to give you all the nutrients essential for good health.

### What Can Happen if I am Overweight?
Being overweight can lead to obesity. Carrying too much weight can make arthritis worse and increase your risk of lifestyle diseases such as diabetes, heart disease, high blood pressure and some cancers.

### Everyone is an Individual
Remember you are an individual. Hereditary factors can influence your natural body shape, weight and height; we can't change this genetic influence. However, we can control our food, exercise and lifestyle habits. These efforts help to manage our weight, fitness and overall health.

### Healthy Eating
Hints to help correct poor eating habits, for better health and weight control.
- Eat your meal slowly and enjoy each mouthful. Chew your food thoroughly. Swallow each mouthful before putting more food on your fork.
- Rest your cutlery between bites of food.
- Increase your fibre intake—plenty of wholegrain cereals, fruit and vegetables.
- Lower your fat intake by trimming the fat off meat and the skin off chicken.
- Include more fish in your diet (not fried of course!). Poached, grilled and oven-baked fish is moist and flavoursome.
- Drink at least 2 litres of fresh water every day.
- Minimise your alcohol intake. Remember, water is best.
- Minimise your confectionery intake.

- Eat regular meals.
- Don't skip out on your breakfast.
- If you are eating between meals, choose low-fat snacks, e.g. fruit.
- Have low-fat dairy products, e.g. low-fat milk, yoghurt and cheese.
- Cut down on cakes, biscuits and pastries.
- Pack your own snacks for morning tea.
- Drink low-joule ('diet') cordial and drinks.
- Follow low-fat cooking principles, e.g. poach, steam, microwave and grill – all without added fat.
- Never skip meals, as there is always a tendency to overeat at the next meal. People who miss meals have a tendency to be overweight.
- Be cautious with the sauces and condiments accompanying your meals. Look for low-fat, flavoursome alternatives.
- Use a smaller size dinner plate.
- Presentation of meals is important. Use low-fat garnishes, herbs and spices where possible.
- Eat meals at regular times to avoid excessive binges.
- Only eat in the dining area, preferably at the table.
- Don't forget the table setting. This creates a pleasant environment for dining.
- Select a wide variety of foods. Vary the types of meat, vegetables and fruits so that meals are not repetitive.
- Avoid shopping when you are hungry.
- Use a shopping list for purchases. This reduces the likelihood of impulse buying.

### Dietary Guidelines for all Australians
Here is a summary of guidelines for healthier eating.
- Enjoy a wide variety of nutritious foods.
- Eat plenty of breads and cereals (preferably wholegrain), vegetables (including legumes) and fruits.
- Eat a diet low in fat and, in particular, low in saturated fat.
- Maintain a healthy body weight by balancing physical activity and food intake.
- If you drink alcohol, limit your intake.
- Eat only a moderate amount of sugars and foods containing added sugars.

- Choose low-salt foods and use salt sparingly.
- Encourage and support breastfeeding.
- Eat foods containing calcium. This is particularly important for girls and women.
- Eat foods containing iron. This is particularly important for girls, women, vegetarians and athletes.

## Fat

Fat is a concentrated form of energy (kilojoules/calories). Lower fat intakes are recommended for children over 5 and adults, especially those who need to limit their kilojoule intake to control body weight. We need to especially aim to minimise our saturated fats, which can cause heart disease. Sometimes fat is 'hidden' in food. Try to decrease the amount of saturated fat in favour of mono-unsaturated fats.

Try to be aware of the major sources of fat in your diet:
- cakes, biscuits and pastries
- fried foods
- greasy, take-away foods
- cheese
- gravy
- cream sauces
- sausages and processed meats
- chicken skin
- visible fat on meat
- cream
- butter and margarine
- snack foods, e.g. potato crisps and corn chips
- chocolate and carob

## Dietary Fibre

How much fibre are you eating? Fibre is found in plant foods such as wholemeal bread, wholegrain cereals, fruits, vegetables, legumes and nuts. Fibre is filling and satisfies hunger for longer, therefore helping in weight control. Your body needs fibre to help prevent constipation, fight cancer, lower cholesterol and manage diabetes.

Some fibre boosting ideas:
- dried beans, peas and lentils, e.g. baked beans, lentil soup, rice

bran added casseroles, four-bean salad
- breads – choose wholegrain, wholemeal and fibre increased varieties
- breakfast cereals – enjoy wholegrain types and add extra bran
- fresh fruits and vegetables – leave skin on where possible for bonus fibre
- nuts – in moderation due to their high fat content

## Calcium

Calcium is vital for strong healthy bones and teeth. Throughout life, our body needs calcium for growth and strength. Later in life, calcium is still needed to maintain bone strength and prevent osteoporosis (porous and brittle bones).

The richest sources of calcium are found in dairy foods like milk, yoghurt and cheese, including low and reduced-fat varieties. Aim for 3 serves of dairy foods each day. A 250 ml (8 oz) glass of milk = 30 g (1 oz) slice/wedge cheese = 200 g (7 oz) yoghurt. Calcium-fortified soy beverages have the same calcium content as regular milk. Moderate amounts of calcium are also found in canned fish with edible bones, green vegetables and almonds.

## Salt

Watch your salt shaker! A high salt (sodium) intake can contribute to high blood pressure. Your body gets all the sodium it needs from the food you consume, without the need to add more. 'Hidden' sources of salt include:
- processed foods
- salt added to home-cooked foods
- take-away foods
- sauces, e.g. soy sauce, tomato sauce
- products like stock cubes
- beef, vegetable and yeast extracts, e.g. Vegemite™
- preserved foods such as olives, anchovies
- processed meats, e.g. bacon, ham and sausages
- cheese and cheese spreads
- canned fish (in brine)

## What About my Alcohol Intake?

Alcohol has no nutritional value and is high in kilojoules (calories). When drinking alcohol, the kilojoules supplied to your body

Bread – Married Loaf (see recipe page 18)

cannot be stored. That is, the alcohol is 'burnt up' as fuel first, and the foods eaten (especially fat) are stored. Alcohol can therefore cause weight gain. Small amounts of alcohol are considered safe. Females can enjoy 2 standard drinks a day and males are recommended to consume no more than 4 standard drinks a day. Don't forget those 2 alcohol-free days each week.

Here are some suggestions for when you are drinking alcohol.

- Alternate your alcohol drink with water or mineral water.
- Have water on the table during every meal.
- Water-down your alcohol with mineral or soda water.
- Have drier, rather than sweeter wines.
- Don't over-consume – you may have to drive home.
- Have one sip of alcohol to one sip of water or mineral water.
- Drink mineral water most of the time and only a little alcohol.

## Eating Out

If eating out is rare, one occasion will not spoil your healthy eating efforts. However, if you entertain or dine out frequently you will need to consider the following suggestions to keep your body weight and health in good control.

- Go to restaurants that have a large variety for you to choose from on the menu.
- Peruse the menu carefully. Avoid dishes that come with fat-laden extras such as side orders of chips.
- Be assertive when ordering. Request alternative low-fat cooking methods and ingredients, e.g. char-grilled fish instead of deep-fried, and skim milk for cappuccino.
- For most people a three-course meal is excessive, so it is best to have one or two courses.
- Remember to choose the lower-fat choices on the menu.
- Avoid garlic or herb breads with lots of butter. Ask for plain dinner rolls, instead.
- Remove any visible fat from food, e.g. chicken skin or meat fat.
- Avoid fried, battered foods.
- When there is a smorgasbord, watch your food intake. It is easy to keep going back and re-filling your plate. One serving (not too large) is enough.
- Limit your alcohol intake.
- Choose dishes without creamy sauces and gravies.
- Fresh fruit and fruit based desserts are ideal if you need more

after you have had your main course.

- Watch how many after-dinner chocolates you have.

## Entrées

- Often entrée-sized serves are appropriate as a main meal, particularly when accompanied by a side order of undressed salad or vegetables plus bread.
- Choose minestrone and vegetable-type soups.
- Choose fresh seafood such as oysters, prawns, mussels, squid, octopus, crab, lobster, trout and salmon. Avoid the deep-fried versions and creamy dressings.
- Choose pasta but avoid the creamy sauces.

## Main

- Seafood and game meats now feature on many menus. Creative cooks are using innovative combinations of herbs and spices to enhance flavour without fat.
- Lean beef, lamb, pork fillets, chicken and turkey are good choices.
- Pasta comes in a variety of sizes and shapes. Avoid cream and butter sauces, choose chunky tomato-based sauces instead, e.g. bolognaise.
- Vegetarian-style dishes are often laden with cream, butter and cheese so choose carefully. If in doubt, ask.

## Desserts

If you feel you want to have dessert, choose fruit-based dishes with low-fat accompaniments. That means forgetting about the high-fat cream and chocolate sauces.

Dessert ideas:

- sauces based on a fruit purée
- filo pastry desserts such as fruit strudel
- if selecting a fruit and cheese platter, try to share it with someone
- sorbet, gelato
- poached fruit
- beware of the having too many after-dinner chocolates

* Commonwealth Department of Health and Family Services 1998, The Australian Guide to Healthy Eating.

# Olden*Days*

## Brawn

Preparation time: 15 minutes
Cooking time: Convection cookery 1 hour

**Ingredients**

6 pigs trotters
1 onion, peeled and finely chopped
1 tablespoon finely chopped parsley
Salt omit salt
Freshly ground black pepper (as desired)

**Method**

1. Place pigs trotters into a large saucepan.
   Barely cover with cold water.
2. Cook over a low temperature until flesh is soft.
3. Remove from heat. Allow to cool slightly.
4. Remove flesh from trotters. Make sure to remove as much
   fat as possible before placing meat into bowl. Place flesh
   into a medium-sized bowl.
5. Add onion, parsley, salt omit salt and pepper.
6. Place a small plate onto top of meat. Place a heavy weight
   onto the plate. Place into refrigerator and allow to set
   overnight or until firm.
7. Next day, remove brawn from bowl and cut into thin slices
   for serving.

## Bubble & Squeak

Serves 4-6
Preparation time: 10 minutes
Cooking time: Convection cookery 5 minutes

**Ingredients**

1 tablespoon butter Use cooking spray to grease pan. When
required use more cooking spray to prevent food from sticking to
the pan
500 g (1 lb) cold cooked diced potatoes
500 g (1 lb) cold cooked shredded cabbage
Salt omit salt
Freshly ground black pepper (as desired)
500 g (1 lb) cold cooked diced beef all fat removed

**Method**

1. Melt half the butter or use cooking spray in a large frying
   pan. Take care not to burn butter.
2. Add potato and cabbage and lightly fry. Add salt omit salt
   and pepper. Set aside and keep hot.
3. Add remainder of butter or use more cooking spray as
   required to pan and fry beef.
4. Place alternate layers of beef and vegetable onto a hot dish,
   piling high in the centre of the dish.

Damper (see recipe below)

Pumpkin Scones (see recipe page 106)

## Damper

Preparation time: 7 minutes
Cooking time: Convection cookery 20 minutes

### Ingredients

3 cups white self-raising flour use 3 cups wholemeal self-raising flour instead of white flour or use half wholemeal self-raising flour and half white self-raising flour

¹/₂ teaspoon salt omit salt

90 g (3 oz) butter 60 g (2 oz) salt-reduced mono-unsaturated margarine

1 cup milk 1 cup low-fat milk

¹/₂ cup water

A little extra milk use a little low-fat milk (for glazing)

### Method

1. Preheat oven to 220°C (425°F).
2. Prepare a flat oven tray by spraying with cooking spray.
3. Sift white flour and salt omit salt into a medium-sized mixing bowl. Add wholemeal flour. Rub butter margarine into dry ingredients with the tips of your fingers until mixture resembles fine breadcrumbs. This process may be done using an electric food processor.
4. Make a well in the centre of the dry ingredients.
5. Combine milk and water. Pour liquid in all at once. Using a table knife, mix to a stiff dough. When substituting wholemeal flour, it may be necessary to add a little more milk to sufficiently moisten dough. Dough should be a stiff consistency.
6. Turn dough out onto a lightly floured board and knead lightly. Knead into a round shape about 5 cm (2 in) high and about 15 cm (6 in) across. Place onto prepared tray. Brush top with a little extra milk.
7. Place into a moderately hot oven and bake for approximately 20 minutes or until golden brown on top and damper sounds hollow in the centre when tapped with the knuckles.
8. Remove from oven and allow to cool on tray for 5 minutes before placing out onto a fine wire rack to cool.

## Gramma Chutney

Gramma (Cucurbita moschate) is a variety of elongated pumpkin (squash) with orange skin and flesh.

Makes 5 x 300 ml (10 oz) jars
Preparation time: 10 minutes
Cooking time: Convection cookery 1 hour

### Ingredients

3 kg (6 lb) gramma
A few cloves
A few peppercorns
1 teaspoon cinnamon
1/2 teaspoon each of mixed spice and cayenne pepper
1.5 kg (3 lb) sugar 1 kg (2 lb) sugar
Brown vinegar

### Method

1. Peel gramma. Remove seeds and cut into 1 cm ($^1/_2$ in) cubes.
2. Tie cloves and peppercorns into a piece of fine muslin cloth.
3. Place all the ingredients into a large saucepan. Nearly cover with vinegar.
4. Cook over a moderate heat for approximately 1 hour or until mixture thickens. Stir occasionally to prevent mixture sticking to the bottom of the saucepan.
5. Remove and discard muslin, cloves and peppercorns.
6. While still warm, bottle in warm sterilised jars and seal.

The reduced-sugar variety will not keep as long and must be stored in the refrigerator.

## Married Loaf

Preparation time: 12 minutes (plus approximately 2 hours for dough to rise)
Cooking time: Convection cookery 45 minutes

### Ingredients

90 g (3 oz) butter 60 g (2 oz) salt-reduced mono-unsaturated margarine or 1 tablespoon canola oil
500 ml (1 pt) milk 500 ml (1 pt) low-fat milk
2 x 7 g ($^1/_4$ oz) sachets dehydrated yeast
1/3 cup sugar $^1/_4$ cup sugar
1 kg (2 lb) white flour 1 kg (2 lb) wholemeal flour
1 teaspoon salt omit salt

### Method

1. Prepare a 30 cm x 12 cm (12 in x 5 in) bread tin by spraying with cooking spray.
2. **Convection cookery**
   Place butter margarine or canola oil into a small saucepan. Add milk and warm gently. Care is necessary not to make the milk too hot or the yeast will not work. or
   **Microwave cookery**
   Place butter margarine or canola oil
   into a small microwave-safe bowl. Cover and microwave on high for 40 seconds or until butter margarine is melted. Add milk and microwave on medium for 40 seconds to warm gently. Care is necessary not to make the milk too hot or the yeast will not work.
3. Place yeast and sugar into a basin and stir well. Gradually stir in warm liquid.
4. Place yeast mixture into a large bowl. Allow to stand for 10 minutes.
5. Sift white flour and salt omit salt into yeast mixture. Stir in wholemeal flour.
   Beat well with a wooden spoon. When substituting wholemeal flour, it may be necessary to add a little more milk to sufficiently moisten mixture. Mixture should be a moist consistency.

6. Cover bowl and allow the dough to prove in a warm place until it doubles in size.
7. Remove dough from bowl onto a lightly floured board. Knead dough for at least 5 minutes until a soft, elastic and pliable dough is achieved.
8. Shape into 2 loaves. Place loaves side-by-side in the prepared tin.
9. Preheat oven to 220°C (425°F).
10. Place bread tin in a warm place and allow bread to prove until it springs back when touched.
11. Place into a hot oven and bake for 15 minutes. Reduce heat to 200°C (400°F) and bake for a further 30 minutes or until golden brown and cooked when tested.
12. Leave bread in tin for 10 minutes before turning out onto a fine wire rack to cool.

## Potato Scones

Makes 12 scones
Preparation time: 10 minutes
Cooking time: Convection cookery 10 minutes

### Ingredients

60 g (2 oz) white self-raising flour 60 g (2 oz) wholemeal self-raising flour
Pinch salt (as desired) omit salt
1 teaspoon baking powder
60 g (2 oz) butter 60 g (2 oz) salt-reduced mono-unsaturated margarine
30 g (1 oz) caster sugar
185 g (6 oz) cooked mashed potato
1 egg, lightly beaten

### Method

1. Preheat oven to 220°C (425°F).
2. Prepare a flat oven tray by spraying with cooking spray.
3. Sift white flour, salt omit salt and baking powder into a medium-sized mixing bowl. Stir in wholemeal flour. Rub butter margarine into dry ingredients with the tips of your fingers until mixture resembles fine breadcrumbs. This process may be done using an electric food processor.
4. Stir in sugar.
5. Mix in potato.
6. Pour in egg and mix to stiff dough. When substituting wholemeal flour, it may be necessary to add a little milk to sufficiently moisten dough. Dough should be a stiff consistency.
7. Shape into 12 portions and place onto prepared tray.
8. Place into a hot oven and bake for approximately 10 minutes or until golden brown and cooked.
9. Allow to cool on tray.

## Salad Dressing

Preparation time: 5 minutes
Cooking time: Convection cookery 10 minutes
Microwave cookery 5 minutes

### Ingredients

**60 g (2 oz) butter** 30 g (1 oz) salt-reduced mono-unsaturated margarine or use 1 tablespoon olive oil

**2 teaspoons mustard**

**1 teaspoon salt** omit salt

**1 cup sugar** $^3/_4$ cup sugar

**3 eggs** use 2 whole eggs and 1 egg white

**1 cup milk** 1 cup low-fat milk

**1 cup white vinegar** with a reduction of sugar, it may be desired to reduce the vinegar to $^3/_4$ cup

### Method

1. **Convection cookery**
   Place butter margarine or oil into a small saucepan and heat gently. Stir in mustard, salt omit salt and sugar. or
   **Microwave cookery**
   Place butter margarine or oil into a medium-sized microwave-safe bowl. Microwave on high for 40 seconds. Stir in mustard, salt omit salt and sugar.

2. Place eggs into a medium-sized bowl and beat lightly. Add milk and mix well. Stir in vinegar.

3. **Convection cookery**
   Pour mixture into saucepan. Cook over a low heat until mixture thickens, stirring continuously. DO NOT BOIL. or
   **Microwave cookery**
   Microwave on high for 1 minute and stir. Continue to microwave on medium-low stirring at 1-minute intervals until mixture thickens. DO NOT BOIL.

4. While still warm, bottle in warm, sterilised jars and seal. Store in the refrigerator. Dressing will keep in the refrigerator for about 3 weeks. When the sugar is reduced the dressing will not keep as long.

# Beef&Lamb

## Baked Lamb with Mint Sauce

Baked lamb with mint sauce served with baked vegetables and fresh garden (or frozen) peas is a very healthy Australian meal. The lamb and mint sauce can be prepared in a healthy way using the recipes below.

To add zest to the meat, slice pockets in the meat and add sprigs of fresh rosemary. Garlic can be used instead of rosemary as desired. The meat will be more succulent if it is basted frequently during cooking. While this was traditionally done with lard, a healthier way of doing it is by using cooking spray. It is important to cook the lamb to your liking. The French prefer lamb rare, while the Arabs like it well done with fruit, particularly apricots. Australians prefer lamb to be tender and succulent. You can serve it as you wish, keeping in mind that it is preferable to cook to slightly underdone rather than overdone.

Mint sauce is the ideal accompaniment to a succulent slice of baked lamb. There are over 40 varieties of mint. It grows profusely and is easy to maintain. If you don't already have some in your garden, try growing some in a pot. It cannot be grown from seed, however a cutting will spread roots rapidly in shaded moist soil. When planted near the kitchen – as all herbs should be – it takes only a matter of minutes to snatch a few leaves, chop them finely and add vinegar and a little sweetener. And there you have mint sauce! The recipe below, however, is a very special one.

Serves 6-8
Preparation time: 20 minutes
Cooking time: Convection cookery 3 hours

### Ingredients
1 x 3 kg (6 lb) leg lamb
2 tablespoons lard omit lard and use cooking spray
$^1/_4$ cup white wine
1 quantity Mint Sauce (see recipe below)

### Method
1. Preheat oven to 160°C (325°F).
2. Prepare a large baking dish by spraying with cooking spray. Place a small wire rack into baking dish. Spray wire rack with cooking spray. Sit leg of lamb onto wire rack. This will allow the fat to run into the bottom of the dish allowing a healthier style of roasting.
3. Place into a moderately slow oven and bake for 2 hours or until meat is cooked. Baste frequently with lard spray frequently with cooking spray and spoons of white wine.
4. Serve with mint sauce (se recipe page 22) baked vegetables and peas.

## Mint Sauce

Mint sauce is best made the day before it is required, to allow the flavour to develop. Store in the refrigerator. It can be used immediately but the flavour will not be as good.

### Ingredients

2 tablespoons red currant jelly (available from supermarkets or speciality stores)
Finely grated rind and juice of 1 orange
1 tablespoon mint, finely chopped
1 tablespoon white vinegar

### Method

1. **Convection cookery**
   Place red currant jelly into a small saucepan. Heat over a gentle heat until jelly is melted. Add rind and orange juice and cook for 1 minute. or
   **Microwave cookery**
   Place red currant jelly into a small microwave-safe bowl.
   Microwave on high for 40 seconds. Add rind and orange juice. Microwave on high for 30 seconds.
2. Add mint to hot liquid. Stir well.
3. Stir in vinegar.
4. Pour immediately into a screw top jar. Seal and leave for 12 hours to allow flavours to develop.

## Beef & Vegetable Soup

This is a thick soup that is suitable for a hearty winter meal.

Serves 6
Preparation time: 15 minutes
Cooking time: Convection cookery 2 hours

### Ingredients

$^1$/₂ cup white flour $^1$/₂ cup wholemeal flour
1 tablespoon gravy stock powder 1 teaspoon reduced-salt gravy stock powder
1 kg (2 lb) chuck steak, cut into 1 cm ($^1$/₂ in) cubes remove all fat from meat
30 g (1 oz) butter use cooking spray to spray pan
2 litres (4 pt) water
$^1$/₂ teaspoon salt omit salt
Freshly ground black pepper (as desired)
2 beef stock cubes use 1 reduced-salt beef stock cube
1 stick celery, finely chopped
1 turnip, peeled and cut into small dice
2 onions, peeled and cut into small dice
2 carrots, peeled and cut into small dice
1 parsnip, peeled and cut into small dice
1 tablespoon pearl barley
1 tablespoon split peas or dried soup mix
1 tablespoon rice bran to increase fibre in the diet

### Method

1. Place flour into a medium-sized bowl. Stir in gravy stock powder. Add meat cubes and toss until well coated.
2. Melt butter spray saucepan with cooking spray in a large saucepan. Cook meat over a high heat until well browned.
3. Remove saucepan from heat and allow to cool slightly.
4. Add water and then remaining ingredients to the saucepan.
5. Simmer with lid on over a gentle heat for approximately 2 hours or until meat is tender. It may be necessary to add a little more stock or water during cooking.

# Beef Stroganoff

Serves 4-6
Preparation time: 10 minutes
Cooking time: Convection cookery 20 minutes

## Ingredients

60 g (2 oz) butter use cooking spray to spray pan
750 g (1 ¹/₂ lb) fillet steak, cut into 1 cm (¹/₂ in) cubes
1 onion, chopped
500 g (1 lb) mushrooms, thinly sliced
Salt omit salt
Freshly ground black pepper (as desired)
1 cup beef stock, made using 1 beef stock cube in 1 cup hot water
use 1 cup home-prepared beef stock (see recipe page 110)
2 tablespoons tomato paste
1 tablespoon cornflour 1 tablespoon rice bran or wholemeal flour
300 ml (¹/₂ pt) sour cream use 300 ml (¹/₂ pt) lite sour cream or
300 ml (¹/₂ pt) natural low-fat yoghurt

## Method

1. Heat half the butter or use cooking spray in a frying pan.
   Pan must be hot but take care not to burn butter.
2. Add half the meat and cook until brown. Remove meat and
   set aside. Repeat with remaining meat.
3. Add remaining butter or use cooking spray to pan. Add
   onion and cook until lightly brown.
4. Add mushrooms and cook until tender.
5. Return meat to pan.
6. Add salt omit salt, pepper and beef stock home-prepared
   beef stock. Stir well to combine.
7. Bring to the boil, reduce heat, cover and cook for 5 minutes.
8. Place tomato paste into a small bowl. Stir in cornflour rice
   bran or wholemeal flour. Stir tomato paste mix into meat
   and mix well. Boil for 1 minute.
9. Gradually add sour cream lite sour cream or natural low-fat
   yoghurt to meat mixture. Reduce heat and simmer gently for
   5 minutes to heat through. DO NOT BOIL. Stir occasionally.

# Casserole Meatballs

Serves 6
Preparation time: 50 minutes
Cooking time: Convection cookery 1¹/₂ – 2 hours

## Ingredients

1 kg (2 lb) mince meat use lean minced beef steak
1 large onion, peeled and finely chopped
³/₄ cup breadcrumbs ³/₄ cup wholemeal breadcrumbs
1 tablespoon rice bran to increase fibre in the diet
Salt omit salt
Freshly ground black pepper (as desired)
2 eggs 1 egg, lightly beaten
Extra flour for tossing meatballs use wholemeal flour
2 tablespoons oil 1 tablespoon olive oil or use cooking spray
2 tablespoons white flour 2 tablespoons wholemeal flour
750 g (24 oz) tomatoes
Boiling water
1 x 850 ml (28 fl oz) can tomato juice no added salt
¹/₂ cup red wine ¹/₃ cup red wine
2 cloves garlic
1 bay leaf

## Method

1. Combine mince, onion, breadcrumbs, rice bran, salt and
   pepper. Add egg. Mix well.
2. Shape into small meatballs.
3. Allow to stand for approximately half an hour.
4. Place flour into a medium-sized bowl. Add meatballs and
   toss until well coated.
5. Heat oil or use cooking spray in a large frying pan. Place
   meatballs into pan. Turn during cooking taking care not to
   break meatballs. (Do not overcrowd during cooking). Cook
   meatballs until well done.
6. Preheat oven to 180°C (350°F).
7. Prepare a medium-sized casserole dish by spraying with
   cooking spray.
8. Remove meatballs from pan and place into casserole dish.
9. Pour excess fat out of pan. Stir 2 tablespoons flour into pan
   drippings and mix well.

Casserole Meatballs (see recipe page 23)

10. Place tomatoes into a medium-sized bowl. Cover with boiling water. Leave for 2 minutes. Remove skins from tomatoes and cut into 1 cm ($^1/_2$ in) dice.
11. Add tomatoes, tomato juice, wine, garlic, salt omit salt and pepper to pan.
12. Cook over a low heat for 5 minutes. Pour sauce over meat balls in casserole dish.
13. Add bay leaf to the sauce.
14. Place into a moderate oven and cook for $1^1/_2$-2 hours. Remove bay leaf before serving. Serve with cooked pasta of your choice. Sprinkle with Parmesan cheese.

Note: This dish can be made ahead of time and reheated. It can also be frozen and reheated when necessary. Care is necessary not to stir the contents of the casserole whilst thawing, as meatballs will break up.

Variations: Grated carrot, grated zucchini or finely chopped parsley can be added to the sauce.

## Chilli Steak

Serves 6
Preparation time: 20 minutes
Cooking time: Convection cookery $1^1/_2$-2 hours

### Ingredients
1 tablespoon oil use cooking spray
750 g ($1^1/_2$ lb) topside steak, cut into 2 cm ($^3/_4$ in) cubes
2 onions, peeled and cut into 1 cm ($^1/_2$ in) cubes
1 carrot, peeled and cut into 1 cm ($^1/_2$ in) cubes
1 potato, peeled and cut into 1 cm ($^1/_2$ in) cubes
1 clove garlic, peeled and crushed
2 teaspoons chilli powder (as desired)
1 teaspoon paprika (as desired)
2 whole cloves
1 bay leaf
Salt omit salt
3 cups beef stock, made using 3 beef stock cubes in 3 cups hot-water use 3 cups home-prepared beef stock (see recipe page 110)
1 x 400 g (14 oz) can whole tomatoes salt-reduced
1 red capsicum, remove seeds and cut into 1 cm ($^1/_2$ in) squares
1 x 400 g (14 oz) can red kidney beans
2 tablespoons white flour 2 tablespoons wholemeal flour

### Method
1. Preheat oven to 160°C (325°F).
2. Prepare a medium-sized casserole dish by spraying with cooking spray.
3. Heat oil or use cooking spray in a large frying pan.
4. Fry meat for approximately 10 minutes or until golden brown. Place into prepared casserole dish.
5. Place onions, carrot, potato and garlic into pan and sauté (lightly fry) for 5 minutes.
6. Add to meat in casserole dish.
7. Mix spices into stock and pour into casserole dish. Add tomatoes.
8. Cover and cook for approximately $1^1/_2$-2 hours
9. Stir capsicum and red kidney beans into casserole.
10. Blend flour with a little cold water. Stir into hot casserole. Cook for a further 5 minutes or until capsicum is cooked.

# Crockpot Casserole

Serves 6
Preparation time: 5 minutes (casserole is best left to marinate overnight)
Cooking time: Convection cookery 6 hours

## Ingredients
6 lamb leg chops cut all fat from chops
I capsicum, cut into rings
I onion, peeled and sliced
I cup tomato paste no added salt
I cup beef stock, made using I beef stock cube in I cup hot water
use I cup home-prepared beef stock (see recipe page 110)
I tablespoon rice bran to increase fibre in the diet
I tablespoon white vinegar
I tablespoon Worcestershire sauce
I tablespoon brown sugar
I teaspoon prepared Dijon mustard
$^1/_2$ teaspoon Tabasco™ sauce
I teaspoon salt omit salt
$^1/_2$ teaspoon freshly ground black pepper (as desired)

## Method
1. Spray inside of crockpot with cooking spray.
2. Place chops into crockpot. Add capsicum and onion slices.
3. Mix remaining ingredients together and pour into crockpot.
4. Cover and marinate overnight.
5. Cook on a very low setting for approximately 6 hours or until meat is tender.

# Crown of Lamb

Serves 6
Preparation time: 20 minutes
Cooking time: Convection cookery $1^1/_4$ hours

## Apple and Raisin Stuffing

### Ingredients
$^1/_4$ loaf fresh bread (approximately 10 slices) wholemeal bread
2 tablespoons soft butter I teaspoon salt-reduced mono-unsaturated margarine
2 tablespoons finely chopped parsley
I cup raisins, finely chopped natural raisins
2 stalks celery, finely chopped
I onion, peeled and finely chopped
I green cooking apple, peeled and finely diced
I teaspoon salt omit salt
$^1/_2$ teaspoon freshly ground black pepper
$^1/_4$ teaspoon dried mixed herbs

### Method
1. Make bread into breadcrumbs. An electric food processor is useful for doing this.
2. Mix butter margarine into breadcrumbs. Mix in remaining ingredients and combine well.

### To assemble
### Ingredients
I crown of lamb (approx. 12 chops)
I quantity apple and raisin stuffing (recipe above)

### Method
1. Preheat oven to 160°C (325°F).
2. Place stuffing into centre of crown.
3. Spray a large baking dish with cooking spray. Place a small wire rack into baking dish. Sit crown of lamb onto wire rack. This will allow the fat to run into the bottom of the pan for a healthier style of roasting.
4. Place into a moderately slow oven and bake for $1^1/_4$ hours or until meat is tender and cooked as desired.

# Curried Mince with Curried Scone Topping

Serves 4-6
Preparation time: 30 minutes
Cooking time: 25 minutes

## Curried Mince

### Ingredients

I teaspoon dripping omit dripping and spray pan with cooking spray

I large onion , peeled and finely diced

I clove freshly crushed garlic

I tablespoon freshly chopped ginger

750 g (1½ lb) lean minced beef

2 teaspoons ground coriander

I teaspoon ground chillies

3 teaspoons paprika

I teaspoon cumin

2 teaspoons turmeric

2 teaspoons curry powder

I tablespoon rice bran to increase fibre in the diet

2 teaspoons sugar

Grated rind and juice I lemon

I x 440 g (15 oz) can tomato soup reduced salt

I cup frozen peas

### Method

1. Melt dripping spray casserole dish with cooking spray in a heavy-duty cook-top casserole dish with a tightly fitting lid.
2. Add onion to casserole dish and increase heat. Brown onion. Add garlic and ginger and stir well. Reduce heat.
3. Add minced beef and cook over a gentle heat until meat is cooked.
4. Add coriander, chilli, paprika, cumin, turmeric, curry power and rice bran and stir well.
5. Add sugar, lemon rind and juice.
6. Add tomato soup and peas and stir well.
7. Remove from heat while preparing Curried Scone Topping (recipe below).

# Curried Scone Topping

### Ingredients

1½ cups white self-raising flour 1½ cups wholemeal self-raising flour

I teaspoon curry powder

I tablespoon lard I tablespoon salt-reduced mono unsaturated margarine

½ cup milk ½ cup low-fat milk

### Method

1. Sift white flour and curry powder into a medium-sized mixing bowl. Stir in wholemeal flour. Rub lard margarine into dry ingredients with the tips of the fingers until mixture resembles fine breadcrumbs. This process may be done using an electric food processor.
2. Make a well in the centre of the dry ingredients. Pour in milk. Use a kitchen knife to stir milk into dry ingredients. Stir from the centre to the outside and mix well. When substituting wholemeal flour, it may be necessary to add a little more milk to sufficiently moisten mixture. Mixture should be a firm consistency.
3. Return casserole dish to heat. Heat over a gentle heat.
4. Turn dough out onto a lightly floured board and knead lightly.
5. Gently pat dough out to 2.5 cm (1 in) thickness.
6. Cut out with a 4 cm (1¼ in) floured cutter to make 12 scones.
7. Place onto curried mince in casserole dish, allowing space for the scones to spread.
8. Cover with lid and gently simmer for 10 minutes.
9. Using 2 teaspoons carefully turn scones over and cook for a further 5 minutes or until cooked when tested.

Goulash (see recipe opposite page)

# Goulash

Serves 6
Preparation time: 20 minutes
Cooking time: Convection cookery 2 hours

## Ingredients

$^1/_2$ cup white flour $^1/_2$ cup wholemeal flour
1 kg (2 lb) blade steak, all fat removed and cut into 1 cm ($^1/_4$in) cubes
2 tablespoons butter 1 tablespoon olive oil or use cooking spray
2 teaspoons paprika
1 kg (2 lb) onions, peeled and finely chopped
2 cloves garlic, peeled and finely sliced
500 g (1 lb) tomatoes
Boiling water
100 ml (3$^1/_2$ oz) red wine
2 cups beef stock, made using 2 beef stock cubes in 2 cups hot water use 2 cups home-prepared beef stock (see recipe page 110)
$^1/_2$ teaspoon dried coriander
Salt omit salt
Freshly ground black pepper (as desired)

## Method

1. Preheat oven to 150°C (300°F).
2. Prepare a medium sized casserole dish by spraying with cooking spray.
3. Place flour into a medium-sized bowl. Add steak cubes and toss until well coated.
4. Melt 1 tablespoon of butter use olive oil or cooking spray in frying pan with 1 teaspoon paprika. Add meat and brown well. Place into prepared casserole dish.
5. Add remaining butter olive oil or cooking spray to frying pan and brown the onion and garlic. Mix in remainder of paprika.
6. Place tomatoes into a medium-sized bowl. Cover with boiling water. Leave for 2 minutes. Remove skins from tomatoes and cut into 1 cm ($^1/_2$ in) dice. Add tomato to frying pan. Simmer over a gentle heat for 5 minutes. Add to meat in casserole dish.
7. Pour wine into casserole dish. Pour in stock to nearly cover the meat (this will be approximately 2 cups).
8. Add coriander and season to taste.
9. Place into a slow oven and cook for approximately 2 hours or until meat is tender.

# Hawaiian Casserole

Most people like the combination of meat and pineapple. This casserole is marinated overnight to develop the flavour. Serve with rice, vegetables or salad as desired.

Serves 4
Preparation time: 10 minutes
Cooking time: Convection cookery 60 minutes
Microwave 40 minutes

## Ingredients

3 tablespoons cornflour 3 teaspoons wholemeal flour
750 g (1$^1/_2$ lb) round steak, cut into 1 cm ($^1/_2$ in) cubes remove all fat from meat
1 x 440 g (15 oz) can pineapple pieces in natural juice
2 tablespoons soy sauce 2 tablespoons salt-reduced soy sauce
1 tablespoon Worcestershire sauce
1 tablespoon brown sugar
1 tablespoon rice bran to increase fibre in the diet
1 tablespoon shredded coconut omit coconut
1 teaspoon Dijon mustard
4 shallots, finely chopped
2 tablespoons pawpaw chutney (or other as desired)
Salt omit salt
Freshly ground black pepper (as desired)
$^1/_2$ cup coconut cream use $^1/_3$ cup lite coconut cream or use $^1/_2$ cup plain natural low-fat yoghurt

## Method

1. Place cornflour wholemeal flour into a medium-sized bowl. Add steak cubes and toss until well coated.
2. Prepare a medium-sized casserole dish by spraying with cooking spray. If you are planning to cook the casserole in

the microwave oven, use a microwave-safe dish.

3. Place all the ingredients, except coconut cream except lite coconut cream or yoghurt into prepared casserole dish.

4. Cover and marinate in the refrigerator over night.

5. **Convection cookery**
   Next day place into a cold oven and set temperature to 150°C (300°F) and cook for 1 hour or until meat is tender. Stir in coconut cream lite coconut cream or yoghurt just before serving. or
   **Microwave cookery**
   Microwave on medium-low for 40 minutes or until meat is tender. Stir in coconut cream lite coconut cream or yoghurt just before serving.

## Meatball Soup

Serves 6-8
Preparation time: 20 minutes
Cooking time: Convection cookery 20 minutes for meatballs + 40 minutes for soup

## Meatballs

### Ingredients

500 g (1 lb) minced steak 500 g (1 lb) lean minced beef
1 onion, peeled and finely chopped
1 egg, lightly beaten
$^1/_2$ cup soft breadcrumbs $^1/_2$ cup soft wholemeal breadcrumbs
1 tablespoon rice bran to increase fibre in the diet
1 tablespoon finely chopped parsley
Freshly ground black pepper (as desired)
$^1/_2$ cup cornflour, approx. wholemeal flour  (for rolling meatballs)
2 tablespoons butter salt-reduced mono-unsaturated margarine or cooking spray

### Method

1. Place minced steak into a medium-sized mixing bowl. Add remaining ingredients – except cornflour wholemeal flour and butter margarine – and mix well.

2. Shape meat mixture into balls the size of a walnut.

3. Place cornflour wholemeal flour into a shallow dish. Roll meatballs in cornflour wholemeal flour.

4. Heat butter margarine in a large saucepan or use cooking spray to coat saucepan.

5. Fry meatballs until golden brown. Drain on absorbent paper.

6. Set meatballs aside while preparing soup.

## Soup

### Ingredients

6 cups beef stock, made using 6 beef stock cubes and 6 cups hot water use home-prepared beef stock (see recipe page 110)
100 g (3$^1/_2$ oz) tomato paste no added salt
1 clove garlic, peeled and crushed
2 onions, peeled and roughly chopped
1 carrot, peeled and cut into small cubes
1 medium sized potato, peeled and cut into small cube
1 x 425 g (14$^1/_2$ oz) can peeled tomatoes no added salt
$^1/_4$ teaspoon freshly ground black pepper
$^1/_2$ teaspoon dried oregano
$^1/_2$ teaspoon dried basil
3 bay leaves
1 cup pasta shells 1 cup wholemeal pasta shells
Freshly grated Parmesan cheese (as desired for serving)

### Method

1. Drain any excess butter margarine from saucepan after cooking meatballs.

2. Place all the ingredients, except meatballs pasta and Parmesan into saucepan.

3. Simmer, with lid on, for 20 minutes.

4. Add meatballs and pasta and simmer for a further 20 minutes.

5. Remove and discard bay leaves.

Serve hot, sprinkled with freshly grated Parmesan cheese.

Meatball Soup (see recipe opposite page)

# Liver & Bacon Casserole

Serves 6
Preparation time: 20 minutes
Cooking time: Convection cookery 1¹/₂ hours

## Ingredients

60 g (2 oz) white flour 60 g (2 oz) wholemeal flour
Salt omit salt
Freshly ground black pepper (as desired)
500 g (1 lb) liver, cut into thin slices
2 tablespoons oil use olive oil and use sparingly
250 g (8 oz) bacon, finely chopped remove all visible fat and rind
2 large onions, peeled and finely chopped
1 x 425 g (14 oz) can tomatoes salt-reduced
450 ml (15 fl oz) tomato juice salt-reduced
¹/₂ teaspoon dried marjoram
1 bay leaf
1 tablespoon Worcestershire sauce
1 cup beef stock, made using 1 beef stock cube in 1 cup hot water
use 1 cup home-prepared beef stock (see recipe page 110)
1 tablespoon rice bran to increase fibre in the diet

## Method

1. Preheat oven to 180°C (350°F).
2. Prepare a large casserole dish with cooking spray.
3. Place flour into a medium-sized bowl. Stir in salt omit salt and pepper. Add liver slices and toss until well coated.
4. Heat oil in a frying pan. Fry liver for approximately 3 minutes on both sides or until golden brown.
5. Remove from frying pan and place into casserole dish.
6. Fry bacon and onions in remaining oil in pan until golden brown. Stir remaining flour into pan.
7. Place tomatoes and juice into pan. Add marjoram, bay leaf, Worcestershire sauce and beef stock. Stir in rice bran.
8. Pour sauce over liver in casserole dish. Mix well.
9. Cover casserole dish. Place into a moderate oven and cook for 1¹/₂ hours or until meat is tender.
10. Taste before serving and adjust seasoning as desired. Remove and discard bay leaf.
11. Reheat just prior to serving.

# Meat Loaf

Serves 6-8
Preparation time: 15 minutes
Cooking time: Convection cookery 1 hour
Microwave cookery 12 minutes

## Ingredients

2 slices bread 2 slices wholemeal bread
¹/₂ cup tomato juice no added salt tomato juice
1 tablespoon rice bran to increase fibre in the diet
250 g (8 oz) sausage mince 250 g (8 oz) finely ground lean beef mince
1 large onion, peeled and finely minced
1 tablespoon parsley, finely chopped
1 stalk celery, finely chopped
¹/₂ teaspoon salt omit salt
Freshly ground black pepper (as desired)
¹/₂ teaspoon each of ground nutmeg, cinnamon & paprika
2 eggs, lightly beaten 1 whole egg and 1 egg white
1 teaspoon lemon juice

## Method

1. Preheat oven to 180°C (350°F).
2. Prepare a 23 cm x 13 cm (9 in x 5 in) loaf tin by spraying with cooking spray.
3. Place bread into a medium-sized bowl. Pour in tomato juice and allow to soak into bread.
4. Combine remaining ingredients and add to bread and tomato juice. Mix well.
5. **Convection cookery**
   Place mixture into prepared loaf tin. Place into a moderate oven and cook for approximately
   1 hour. Allow to cool in tin until required for serving. or
   **Microwave cookery**
   Place mixture into an oiled ring-shaped microwave-safe mould. Microwave on high for
   approximately 12 minutes or until cooked. Allow to cool in mould until required for serving.
   Serve slices hot or cold as desired.

## Mutton Pie

Serves 6
Preparation time: 30 minutes
Cooking time: Convection cookery $1^1/_2$ hours for meat and 50 minutes for baking the pie

## Mutton Filling

### Ingredients

I cup white flour I cup wholemeal flour
$1^1/_2$ kg (3 lb) mutton, cut into I cm ($^1/_2$ in) cubes
90 g (3 oz) butter 3 teaspoons olive oil or use cooking spray
3 onions, peeled and cut into I cm ($^1/_2$ in) cubes
2 cups water
$^1/_2$ teaspoon salt omit salt
$^1/_4$ teaspoon freshly ground black pepper
I tablespoon Worcestershire sauce
I tablespoon tomato sauce no added salt
I tablespoon rice bran to increase fibre in the diet

### Method

1. Place flour into a medium-sized bowl. Add meat cubes and toss until well coated.
2. Heat 30 g (1 oz) butter I teaspoon olive oil or use cooking spray in a large saucepan.
3. Put half the meat into saucepan and fry quickly until brown.
4. Remove meat from saucepan and repeat with remaining meat and 30 g (1 oz) butter I teaspoon olive oil or use cooking spray.
5. Fry onion in the saucepan with remaining butter olive oil or cooking spray.
6. Return meat to saucepan with water, salt omit salt, pepper, Worcestershire sauce, tomato sauce and rice bran.
7. Simmer for approximately $1^1/_2$ hours or until meat is tender.

## Pastry

### Ingredients

3 cups white flour $1^1/_2$ cups white flour and $1^1/_2$ cups wholemeal flour
I teaspoon baking powder
$^1/_2$ teaspoon salt omit salt
125 g (4 oz) butter 90 g (3 oz) salt-reduced mono-unsaturated margarine
150 ml (5 fl oz) water
I teaspoon lemon juice
I egg yolk omit egg yolk
I egg, lightly beaten (for glazing) omit egg and use 2 tablespoons low-fat milk

### Method

1. Preheat oven to 220°C (425°F).
2. Prepare a deep 20 cm (11 in) pie dish by spraying with cooking spray.
3. Sift white flour, baking powder and salt omit salt into a medium-sized mixing bowl. Stir in wholemeal flour. Rub butter margarine into dry ingredients with the tips of the fingers until mixture resembles fine breadcrumbs. This process may be done using an electric food processor.
4. Pour water and lemon juice into a jug. Add egg yolk omit egg yolk and mix well. Pour into flour mixture and mix to a firm dough. When substituting wholemeal flour, it may be necessary to add a little more water to sufficiently moisten dough. Dough should be a firm consistency.
5. Turn dough onto a lightly floured board and knead lightly.
6. Reserve about $^1/_3$ of the dough for top of pie. Roll remainder of dough to 0.5 cm ($^1/_4$ in) thickness.
7. Cut pastry out to 5 cm (2 in) larger than pie dish. Line prepared dish with pastry.
8. Place cold meat mixture into pie dish.
9. Dip glazing brush in water, moisten edges of pastry.
10. Roll remainder of dough to $^1/_2$ cm ($^1/_4$ in) thickness.
11. Cover meat with pastry. Press edges of pastry lightly together. Trim excess pastry. Decorate top of pie with any remaining pastry. Decorate edges of pie. Make a small slit in

the top of the pastry for steam to escape during baking.

12. Glaze with egg omit egg and use milk.

13. Place into a hot oven and bake for 10 minutes. Reduce heat to 180°C (350°F) and bake for a further 40 minutes or until pastry is cooked as desired. Take care not to burn pastry during cooking.

## Party Pies

These party pies are suitable to have before a barbecue. They can be served warm or cold as desired.

Makes approximately 20 pies (depending on size of trays used)
Preparation time: 20 minutes
Cooking time: Convection cookery 12-15 minutes

## Meat Filling

### Ingredients

2 teaspoons olive oil I teaspoon olive oil or use cooking spray to spray frying pan
1 onion, peeled and finely chopped
1 clove garlic, peeled and crushed
500 g (1 lb) minced beef 500 g (1 lb) lean minced beef
Freshly ground black pepper (as desired)
1 tablespoon Worcestershire sauce
1 tablespoon tomato sauce no added salt
I tablespoon rice bran to increase fibre in the diet
1 tablespoon finely chopped parsley
$^1/_4$ teaspoon ground nutmeg
2 rashers bacon all fat and rind removed finely chopped

### Method

1. Heat oil in a frying pan. Or use cooking spray, to spray frying pan.
2. Add onion and garlic and sauté (lightly fry).
3. Add meat to pan and cook as desired. (Do not overcook.)
4. Add pepper, Worcestershire sauce, tomato sauce, rice bran, parsley and nutmeg.
5. **Convection cookery**
   Grill bacon under a moderately hot griller. or
   **Microwave cookery**
   Place bacon onto absorbent paper on a microwave-safe

plate. Cover with 2 thicknesses of paper. Microwave on high for 1 minute. Turn and microwave for a further 1 minute or until cooked as desired.

6. Add cooked bacon to meat in pan and mix well.

## Pastry

### Ingredients

3 cups white flour I cup white flour and 2 cups wholemeal flour
$^1/_2$ teaspoon baking powder
$^1/_2$ teaspoon salt omit salt
125 g (4 oz) butter 90 g (3 oz) salt-reduced mono-unsaturated margarine
150 ml (5 fl oz) water
1 teaspoon lemon juice
1 egg yolk omit egg yolk
1 egg, lightly beaten (for glazing) omit egg and use 2 tablespoons low-fat milk

### Method

1. Preheat oven to 200°C (400°F).
2. Individual, 6 cm ($2^1/_2$ in) foil trays are best for these pies.
3. Sift white flour, baking powder and salt omit salt into a medium-sized mixing bowl. Stir in wholemeal flour. Rub butter margarine into dry ingredients with the tips of the fingers until mixture resembles fine breadcrumbs. This process may be done using an electric food processor.
4. Pour water and lemon juice into a jug. Add egg yolk omit egg yolk and mix well. Pour into flour mixture and mix to a firm dough. When substituting wholemeal flour, it may be necessary to add a little more water to sufficiently moisten dough. Dough should be a firm consistency.
5. Turn dough out onto a lightly floured board and knead lightly. Roll dough to 0.5 cm ($^1/_4$ in) thickness. Cut out 6.5 cm ($2^1/_2$ in) rounds of pastry. Carefully place into foil trays.
6. Add one tablespoon of meat filling to each pie shell.
7. Top with a 4 cm (2 in) circle of pastry.
8. Place pies onto an oven tray.
9. Glaze with egg omit egg and use milk.
10. Place into a moderately hot oven and bake for approximately 12-15 minutes or until golden brown.

Party Pies (see recipe opposite page)

# Pasties

Makes 12
Preparation time: 30 minutes
Cooking time: Convection cookery 20 minutes

## Filling

### Ingredients

1 large potato, peeled and finely grated
1 large carrot, peeled and finely grated
1 large onion, peeled and finely grated
500 g (1 lb) mince meat lean minced beef
1 tablespoon Worcestershire sauce
1 tablespoon tomato sauce no added salt
1 tablespoon rice bran to increase fibre in the diet
$^1/_2$ teaspoon salt omit salt
$^1/_2$ teaspoon freshly ground black pepper (as desired)

### Method

1. Mix prepared vegetables with meat and stir in sauces and rice bran. Season with salt omit salt and pepper.

# Pastry

### Ingredients

3 cups white flour 1 cup white flour and 2 cups wholemeal flour
1 teaspoon baking powder
$^1/_4$ teaspoon salt omit salt
155 g (5 oz) butter 125 g (4 oz) salt-reduced mono-unsaturated margarine
3 tablespoons water
1 teaspoon lemon juice
1 egg yolk omit egg yolk
1 egg, lightly beaten (for glazing) omit egg and use 2 tablespoons low-fat milk

### Method

1. Preheat oven to 200°C (400°F).
2. Prepare a flat oven tray by spraying with cooking spray.
3. Sift white flour, baking powder and salt omit salt into a medium-sized mixing bowl. Stir in wholemeal flour. Rub butter margarine into dry ingredients with the tips of the fingers, until mixture resembles fine breadcrumbs. This process may be done using an electric food processor.
4. Pour water and lemon juice into a jug. Add egg yolk omit egg yolk and mix well. Pour into flour mixture and mix to a firm dough. When substituting wholemeal flour, it may be necessary to add a little more water to sufficiently moisten dough. Dough should be a firm consistency.
5. Turn dough out onto a lightly floured board and knead lightly. Roll dough out to 0.5 cm ($^1/_4$ in) thickness.
6. Cut into circles using a saucer and small sharp knife.
7. Place a tablespoon of filling mixture onto the centre of each circle.
8. Using a glazing brush dipped in water, moisten edges of pastry circles. Fold in half.
9. Place onto prepared tray. Flute top of pasties. Glaze with egg omit egg and use milk.
10. Place into a moderately hot oven and bake for approximately 20 minutes or until golden brown and cooked.

Pasties (see recipe opposite page)

# Roast Beef & Gravy

Preparation time: 12 minutes
Cooking time: Convection cookery 1¹/₂ hours approximately for beef

## Ingredients

1 x 2 kg (4 lb) rolled roast of beef make sure you purchase a lean piece of beef
2 cloves garlic, peeled and cut into thin slivers
2 tablespoons dripping spray beef with cooking spray
1 tablespoon white flour 1 tablespoon wholemeal flour (use 2 tablespoons flour if you prefer a thick gravy)
2 cups beef stock, made using 2 beef stock cubes in 2 cups hot water use home-prepared beef stock (see recipe page 110)

## Method

1. Preheat oven to 160°C (325°F).
2. Make regular slits in beef with a sharp pointed knife.
3. Insert a sliver of garlic in each slit in beef.
4. Place beef into baking dish, fat side uppermost. Place dripping into baking dish omit dripping and spray baking dish and beef with cooking spray. Beef may be raised from base of dish on a wire trivet if desired. This will allow fat to drain from meat and convection currents to circulate around beef during roasting. Roast the beef in a moderately slow oven for 1 1/2 hours or until beef is cooked as desired. Turn beef frequently during roasting to allow juices to flow evenly throughout meat. Take care when turning beef not to pierce beef and let juices escape. Best results will be obtained by basting with baking dish juices each time the meat is turned.
5. When cooked as desired, remove from baking dish.
6. Wrap in foil for 20 minutes before carving to allow heat to equalise. Roast will remain hot for up to half an hour.
7. Strain any excess fat from baking dish. Stir flour into baking dish juices.
8. Gradually add stock to baking dish, stirring well to mix in flour.
9. Place baking dish over source of heat and cook stirring continuously until mixture boils and thickens.

Serve roast beef and gravy with Yorkshire pudding (see recipe on page 117) and baked vegetables. Spray vegetables with cooking spray and dry roast.

# Sausage Pie

Sausages have been a favourite economical food in many homes. This recipe uses the humble sausage in a very tasty way.

Serves 6
Preparation time: 30 minutes
Cooking time: Convection cookery 40 minutes

## Sausage Filling

### Ingredients

10 thin sausages use fat-reduced sausages
1 onion, peeled and finely chopped
2 eggs, lightly beaten
1 teaspoon crushed garlic
1 cup evaporated milk 1 cup reduced-fat evaporated milk
1 slice bread 1 slice wholemeal bread
¹/₃ cup Parmesan cheese ¹/₄ cup Parmesan cheese

### Method

1. Prepare sausages by placing into a large saucepan. Cover with water and bring gently to the boil. Strain water. Remove skins from sausages.

## Pastry

### Ingredients

2 cups white flour 1 cup white flour and 1 cup wholemeal flour
¹/₂ teaspoon baking powder
¹/₂ teaspoon salt omit salt
100 g (3¹/₂ oz) butter 60 g (2 oz) salt-reduced mono-unsaturated margarine
100 ml (3¹/₂ oz) water
1 teaspoon lemon juice
1 egg yolk omit egg yolk

**Method**

1. Preheat oven to 180°C (350°F).
2. Prepare a 23 cm (9 in) flat pie dish by spraying with cooking spray.
3. Sift white flour, baking powder and salt omit salt into a medium-sized mixing bowl. Stir in wholemeal flour. Rub butter margarine into dry ingredients with the tips of the fingers until mixture resembles fine breadcrumbs. This process may be done using an electric food processor.
4. Pour water and lemon juice into a jug. Add egg yolk omit egg yolk and mix well. Pour into flour mixture and mix to a firm dough. When substituting wholemeal flour, it may be necessary to add a little more water to sufficiently moisten dough. Dough should be a firm consistency.
5. Turn dough out onto a lightly floured board and knead lightly. Roll dough out to 0.5 cm ($^1/_4$ in) thickness. Line base of pie dish with pastry. Any remaining pastry can be kept and used to decorate top of pie.

**To assemble**

1. Place sausages onto pastry in pie dish.
2. Place onion, egg, garlic and evaporated milk into the bowl of an electric food blender. Blend until smooth. Pour over sausages.
3. Decorate top of pie with remaining pastry.
4. Make fine breadcrumbs with the slice of bread. This can be easily done by using a food processor or blender.
5. Mix Parmesan cheese into breadcrumbs. Sprinkle over top of pie.
6. Place into a moderate oven and bake for approximately 40 minutes or until set in the centre when tested.

## Steak & Kidney Pie

Serves 4-6
Preparation time: 25 minutes
Cooking time: Convection cookery 1$^1/_2$ hours to cook meat + 30 minutes to cook pie

## Steak & Kidney Filling

**Ingredients**

1 sheep's kidney
Freshly ground black pepper (as desired)
250 g (8 oz) rump steak, cut into 1 cm ($^1/_2$ in) cubes all fat removed
1 tablespoon white flour 1 tablespoon wholemeal flour
1 tablespoon rice bran to increase fibre in the diet

**Method**

1. Wash kidney. Remove skin and cut into 1 cm ($^1/_2$ in) cubes.
2. Place flour into a medium-sized bowl. Stir in pepper. Add steak and kidney and toss until well coated. Stir in rice bran.
3. Place meat into a medium-sized saucepan. Add just enough water to cover meat. Cook over a gentle heat with lid on until meat is tender, approximately 1$^1/_2$ hours. Allow to cool.

## Pastry

**Ingredients**

2 cups white flour 1 cup white flour and 1 cup wholemeal flour
$^1/_2$ teaspoon baking powder
$^1/_2$ teaspoon salt omit salt
100 g (3$^1/_2$ oz) butter 90 g (3 oz) salt-reduced mono-unsaturated margarine
100 ml (3$^1/_2$ fl oz) water
1 teaspoon lemon juice
1 egg yolk omit egg yolk
1 egg, lightly beaten (for glazing) omit egg and use 2 tablespoons low-fat milk

## Method

1. Preheat oven to 220°C (425°F).
2. Prepare a deep 20 cm (11 in) pie dish by spraying with cooking spray.
3. Sift white flour, baking powder and salt omit salt into a medium-sized mixing bowl. Stir in wholemeal flour.
4. Rub butter margarine into dry ingredients with the tips of the fingers until mixture resembles fine breadcrumbs. This process may be done using an electric food processor.
5. Pour water and lemon juice into a jug. Add egg yolk omit egg yolk and mix well. Pour into flour mixture and mix to a firm dough. When substituting wholemeal flour, it may be necessary to add a little more water to sufficiently moisten dough. Dough should be a firm consistency.
6. Turn dough out onto a lightly floured board and knead lightly.
7. Roll dough out to $^1/_2$ cm ($^1/_4$ in) thickness.
8. Cut pastry top out to 5 cm (2 in) larger than pie dish and set aside.
9. Cut a strip of pastry 1 cm ($^1/_2$ in) wide and place around rim of pie dish. Brush pastry strip with water.
10. Place cold meat mixture into prepared pie dish.
11. Cover meat with pastry top. Press edges of pastry lightly together. Trim excess pastry. Decorate top of pie with any remaining pastry. Decorate edges of pie. Make a small slit in the top of the pastry for steam to escape during baking.
12. Glaze with egg omit egg and use milk.
13. Place into a hot oven and bake for 10 minutes. Reduce heat to 180°C (350°F) and bake for a further 20 minutes or until pastry is cooked as desired. Take care not to burn pastry during cooking.

## Shepherd's Pie

Serves 6
Preparation time: 20 minutes
Cooking time: Convection cookery 40 minutes

### Ingredients

6 large potatoes
2 tablespoons milk approx. (for mashing potato) low-fat milk
1 tablespoon butter (for mashing potato) omit butter
Salt (for mashing potato) omit salt
Freshly ground black pepper (as desired, for mashing potato)
500 g (1 lb) cold, diced, baked lamb, finely minced use lean lamb and remove all fat
1 onion, peeled and finely chopped
$^1/_2$ teaspoon dried mixed herbs
1 tablespoon finely chopped parsley
1 teaspoon salt omit salt
$^1/_2$ teaspoon freshly ground black pepper
$^1/_4$ teaspoon ground nutmeg
1 tablespoon rice bran to increase fibre in the diet
2 tablespoons tomato relish 2 tablespoons reduced-salt tomato relish
1 rasher bacon all fat and rind removed
$^1/_2$ cup grated cheddar cheese $^1/_3$ cup grated reduced-fat cheddar cheese
1 egg omit egg

### Method

1. Preheat oven to 200°C (400°F).
2. Prepare a 25 cm (10 in) pie dish by spraying with cooking spray.
3. Peel potatoes and cut into small cubes. Place into boiling salted water and cook until potato is soft. Place potato cubes into the top of a steamer and steam without salt until potato is soft. Drain and mash with a little milk, butter, salt and pepper use skim milk and omit butter and salt.
4. Line bottom of pie dish with mashed potato.
5. Combine meat, onion, herbs, salt, omit salt pepper, nutmeg, rice bran and tomato relish and mix well.
6. Place seasoned meat onto potato in pie dish.

Shepperd's Pie (see recipe opposite page)

7. Place the remainder of the mashed potato on top of the meat.
8. Cut bacon into long thin strips and place across the potato.
9. Sprinkle with grated cheese.
10. Beat egg omit egg and pour over the cheese.
11. Place into a moderate to hot oven and bake for approximately 40 minutes or until heated through and golden brown on top.

## Stir-fry Beef & Almonds

Serves 2-3
Preparation time: 30 minutes
Cooking time: Convection cookery 7 minutes
Rice may be cooked ahead of time and stored in a covered container in the refrigerator until required.

### Ingredients

1 cup white rice 1 cup brown rice
1 cup boiling water
250 g (8 oz) rump steak, cut into thin strips all fat removed
3 teaspoons cornflour
$\frac{1}{2}$ teaspoon ground ginger
3 teaspoons dripping 3 teaspoons macadamia oil, canola oil or olive oil, or use cooking spray
125 g (4 oz) whole blanched almonds 90 g (3 oz) whole blanched almonds
1$\frac{1}{2}$ teaspoons grated fresh ginger
1 clove garlic, peeled and crushed
$\frac{1}{2}$ cup thin strips butternut pumpkin
125 g (4 oz) broccoli florets, cut into small pieces
2 tablespoons soy sauce 2 tablespoons reduced-salt soy sauce
1 teaspoon sugar
1 tablespoon sherry

### Method

1. **Convection cookery**
   Place rice into a medium-sized saucepan. Pour boiling water over rice. Cook with lid off over a gentle heat for approximately 7 minutes or until rice is tender. Rice can be cooked in a rice cooker or steamer as desired. Strain, cover rice and set aside while preparing beef. or
   **Microwave cookery**
   Place rice into a medium-sized microwave-safe bowl. Pour boiling water over rice. Microwave on medium-high for approximately 5 minutes or until rice is tender. Rice can be cooked in a microwave rice cooker. Cover and set aside while preparing beef.
2. Place beef strips into a large mixing bowl. Add cornflour and ground ginger and toss throughout meat. Cover and set aside.
3. Heat 2 teaspoons dripping oil or cooking spray in a wok.
4. Add almonds and stir continuously until a pale golden colour. Remove almonds from wok and set aside.
5. Add remaining 1 teaspoon dripping oil or cooking spray to the wok. Add fresh ginger and garlic and stir-fry for approximately 1 minute.
6. Add beef strips and stir-fry until beef is medium-rare. (Cook more if desired, but do not over-cook.)
7. Add butternut pumpkin strips. Stir-fry for approximately 2 minutes or until just tender.
8. Add broccoli and stir-fry until it becomes a bright colour. (Take care not to over-cook broccoli.)
9. Mix soy sauce, sugar and sherry together in a small jug. Pour into wok. Stir-fry for approximately 1 minute until sauces are mixed in.
10. Return almonds to wok. Stir for approximately 1 minute.
11. Remove immediately from wok and serve on a bed of cooked rice.

Stir-fry Beef Almonds (see recipe opposite page)

## Sweet Curry

This curry has a delicious fruity flavour. You can make it hotter to your liking by adding stronger mustard and more curry if you wish. Serve on a bed of rice sprinkled with chopped parsley and wedges of lemon. Rice can be cooked ahead of time.

This recipe has no added fat and is well suited to a low-fat diet.

Serves 6
Preparation time: 20 minutes
(Meat is best marinated overnight to develop flavour.)
Cooking time: Convection cookery 40 minutes
Microwave cookery 50 minutes

### Ingredients

2 tablespoons maize cornflour

1 kg (2 lb) lean veal, cut into 1 cm (¹/₂ in) cubes remove any visible fat from veal

¹/₃ cup chopped dried apricots use natural dried apricots, they will be darker in colour due to the absence of sulfur in the drying process, but have a better flavour

¹/₃ cup sultanas use 'no natural oil' sultanas

¹/₃ cup chopped raisins natural raisins

¹/₄ cup chopped shallots

2 teaspoons prepared Mild mustard

1 teaspoon curry powder

¹/₂ cup sweet white wine ¹/₂ cup dry white wine

2 teaspoons Worcestershire sauce

1 tablespoon soy sauce 1 tablespoon reduced-salt soy sauce

1 tablespoon honey

1 tablespoon rice bran to increase fibre in the diet

### Method

1. Prepare a large (Pyrex®) casserole dish by spraying with cooking spray.

2. Place cornflour into a medium-sized bowl. Add veal cubes and toss until well coated. Place into prepared casserole dish.

3. Place apricots, sultanas, raisins and shallots over veal cubes in casserole dish.

4. Mix mustard, curry, wine, sauces and honey in a small bowl. Stir in rice bran. Pour into casserole dish.

5. Cover and marinate in refrigerator overnight.

6. **Convection cookery**

   Next day place curry into a cold oven. Turn oven to 180°C (350°F) and cook for approximately 40 minutes or until veal is tender. Stir once during cooking.

   **Microwave cookery**

   Next day place curry into microwave oven. Microwave on low for approximately 50 minutes or until veal is tender. Stir once during cooking.

   (Although it takes longer to cook the casserole when using the microwave oven, there are the advantages of using less power and easier washing-up to consider.)

# Chicken&Pork

## Apricot Chicken

Serves 6
Preparation time: 7 minutes
Cooking time: Convection cookery 40 minutes
Microwave cookery 30 minutes

Apricot Chicken is served on a bed of cooked rice. Rice brown rice may be cooked ahead of time and stored in a covered container in the refrigerator until required.

### Ingredients

¹/₄ cup white flour (for coating chicken pieces) ¹/₄ cup wholemeal flour
1.5 kg (3 lb) chicken fillets, cut into 3 cm (1¹/₄ in) pieces all skin and fat removed
Salt omit salt
¹/₂ teaspoon pepper
1 x 425 ml (14¹/₂ fl oz) can apricot nectar
1 packet French onion soup 1 packet salt-reduced French onion soup

### Method

1. Preheat oven to 180°C (350°F).
2. Prepare a large (Pyrex®) casserole dish by spraying with cooking spray.
3. Place flour into a medium-sized bowl. Stir in salt omit salt and pepper. Add chicken pieces and toss until well coated. Place chicken into casserole dish.
4. Pour apricot nectar into a medium-sized bowl. Add French onion soup mix and mix well.
5. Convection cookery
   Pour into a medium-sized saucepan and place over a low heat. Bring to the boil, stirring occasionally to prevent sticking. Pour over chicken in casserole dish. Place into a moderate oven and bake for approximately 40 minutes or until chicken is cooked. or
   Microwave cookery Place into a microwave-safe bowl. Microwave on high for approximately 5 minutes, stirring after each minute until mixture thickens. Pour over chicken in casserole dish. Microwave on medium-high for approximately 30 minutes or until chicken is cooked. Serve on a bed of cooked rice brown rice. Garnish with finely chopped parsley.

## Chicken Chow Mein

Serves 6
Preparation time: 20 minutes (Allow 1 hour to marinate chicken. Chicken can be prepared immediately, however the standing time is recommended to allow the flavours to develop.)
Cooking time: Convection cookery 20 minutes

### Ingredients

1 tablespoon cornflour
Salt omit salt
1.5 kg (3 lb) chicken fillets, cut into 2.5 cm (1 in) cubes all skin and fat removed
1 tablespoon soy sauce 1 tablespoon salt-reduced soy sauce
1 tablespoon dry sherry
4 tablespoons oil omit oil and use cooking spray to spray pan

1 clove garlic, peeled and crushed

2.5 cm (1 in) piece green ginger, finely chopped

250 g pork use lean pork, cut into 2.5 cm (1 in) cubes

500 g (1 lb) green paradise prawns, shell prawns and remove veins

2 medium onions, peeled and cut into small cubes

1 red capsicum, remove seeds and cut into small dice

2 sticks celery, chopped into small pieces

1/4 cabbage, finely shredded

1/2 cup chopped shallots

1 teaspoon cornflour (extra)

1/2 cup cold water

1 tablespoon soy sauce 1 tablespoon salt-reduced soy sauce (extra)

1 tablespoon dry sherry (extra)

2 chicken stock cubes use 1 reduced-salt chicken stock cube

250 g (8 oz) crisp noodles of your choice (use instant noodles that do not require cooking)

## Method

1. Place cornflour into a medium-sized bowl. Stir in salt omit salt. Add chicken and toss until well coated. Pour in soy sauce and sherry and mix well. Stand for 1 hour to allow flavours to develop.

2. Heat 2 tablespoons oil in a wok or large frying pan or spray wok or frying pan with cooking spray. Add garlic and ginger and cook for 1 minute.

3. Add remaining oil to wok or frying pan. Add chicken and pork and cook until meat is cooked.

4. Add prawns and cook for a further 5 minutes or until prawns are cooked.

5. Add prepared vegetables to wok or frying pan. Cook for 1 minute, stirring constantly.

6. Place extra cornflour into a small mixing bowl. Gradually stir in water, extra soy sauce and extra sherry and blend well. Mix in stock cubes use 1 stock cube.

7. Pour sauce into wok or frying pan and stir until sauce boils and thickens.

8. To serve – place a ring of noodles onto a large serving plate. Spoon the chicken and vegetables into the centre of the noodles.

# Ham Steaks

Serves 4

Preparation time: 10 minutes

Cooking time: Convection cookery 10 minutes

Microwave cookery 7 minutes

## Ingredients

4 ham steaks

Salt omit salt

Freshly ground black pepper (as desired)

1 teaspoon finely chopped fresh dill

1 tablespoon soy sauce 1 tablespoon salt-reduced soy sauce

1 tablespoon barbecue sauce 1 tablespoon salt-reduced barbecue sauce

1/2 teaspoon dry mustard

Finely grated rind and juice of 1 orange

1 tablespoon cornflour

## Method

1. Season steaks with salt omit salt and pepper as desired.

2. **Convection cookery**
   Spray a large frying pan with cooking spray. Cook steaks over a low heat turning a couple of times during cooking. or
   **Microwave cookery**
   Heat a microwave browning dish in the microwave oven for 5 minutes. Carefully spray dish with cooking spray. Place steaks onto browning dish and microwave on high for 3 minutes. Turn over and microwave for 3 minutes.

3. **Convection cookery**
   Place dill, soy sauce, barbecue sauce, mustard, finely grated orange rind and juice into a small saucepan. Bring to the boil. Reduce heat and simmer for 1 minute. In a separate bowl, blend cornflour with a little cold water. Pour into hot sauce. Bring to the boil and cook for one minute stirring continuously. or
   **Microwave cookery**
   Place dill, soy sauce, barbecue sauce, mustard, finely grated orange rind and juice into a small microwave-safe bowl. Microwave on high for 2 minutes. In a separate

Chicken Chow Mein (see recipe page 45)

bowl, blend cornflour with a little cold water. Pour into hot sauce. Microwave on high for 1 minute and stir – repeat.

4. Pour sauce over steaks.

## Lemon Chicken

Serves 4-6
Preparation time: 7 minutes
Cooking time: Convection cookery 30 minutes
Microwave cookery 25 minutes

### Ingredients

1 medium sized chicken
3 tablespoons olive oil or use cooking spray
$^1/_2$ cup dry white wine
2 teaspoons finely grated lemon rind
$^1/_4$ cup lemon juice
1 teaspoon salt omit salt
Freshly ground black pepper (as desired)
$1^1/_2$ cups chicken stock, made using 2 chicken stock cubes in $1^1/_2$ cups boiling water use home-prepared chicken stock (see recipe page 113)

### Method

1. Preheat oven to 180°C (350°F).
2. Prepare a large (Pyrex®) casserole dish by spraying with cooking spray. Place chicken into dish.
3. Pour oil over chicken in casserole dish. Reduce the amount of oil used and brush chicken with a little olive oil. Place into a moderate oven and bake for 20 minutes. Combine remaining ingredients and pour over chicken. Reduce heat to 160°C (325°F) and bake for a further 10 minutes or until chicken is cooked. or

### Microwave cookery

Pour oil over chicken in microwave-safe casserole dish. Reduce the amount of oil used and brush chicken with a little olive oil. Microwave on medium-high for 20 minutes. Combine remaining ingredients and pour over chicken. Microwave on medium-high for a further 5 minutes or until chicken is cooked. Serve with rice.

## Sweet & Sour Pork

Serves 6
Preparation time: 15 minutes + minimum of 1 hour to marinate meat. (Meat is best if it can be left to marinate overnight.)
Cooking time: Convection cookery 20 minutes

### Ingredients

1 tablespoon sugar 1 teaspoon sugar
2 tablespoons soy sauce 2 tablespoons salt-reduced soy sauce
1 tablespoon dry sherry
1 egg yolk omit egg yolk
1.25 kg ($2^1/_2$ lb) pork pieces, cut into 2 cm ($^3/_3$ in) cubes use lean pork
$^1/_2$ cup (approx.) cornflour (for tossing meat cubes)
6 tablespoons olive oil (for frying meat cubes) cooking spray
1 large onion, peeled and sliced
8 shallots, chopped
1 red capsicum, remove seeds and thinly slice
125 g (4 oz) mushrooms, chopped
1 continental cucumber, sliced
2 sticks celery, sliced into 1 cm ($^1/_2$ in) slices
1 x 440 g (14 oz) can pineapple pieces in natural juice
2 tablespoons soy sauce (extra) 2 tablespoons salt-reduced soy sauce
2 tablespoons tomato sauce 2 tablespoons salt-reduced tomato sauce
$^1/_4$ cup white vinegar
1 cup beef stock, made using 1 beef stock cube in 1 cup hot water use home-prepared beef stock (see recipe page 110)
$1^1/_2$ tablespoons cornflour (extra)

### Method

1. Place sugar, soy sauce, sherry and egg yolk omit egg yolk into a medium-sized mixing bowl. Add meat and stir well. Cover and marinate for 1 hour or overnight if desired.
2. Drain meat and reserve any liquid.
3. Place cornflour into a medium-sized bowl. Add meat cubes and toss until well coated.

4. Heat 2 tablespoons oil in a large frying pan or spray pan with cooking spray. Add half the meat cubes and cook until golden brown. Drain meat cubes on absorbent paper. Add 2 more tablespoons oil or spray pan with cooking spray to pan and cook remaining meat cubes. Drain meat cubes on absorbent paper.

5. Add 2 tablespoons oil to pan or spray pan with cooking spray. Add the prepared vegetables. Sauté (lightly fry) for 3 minutes.

6. Strain juice from pineapple into a medium-sized jug. Pour in reserved marinade from meat. Pour extra soy sauce, tomato sauce, vinegar and beef stock into jug.

7. Place extra cornflour into a medium-sized bowl. Blend with a little liquid. Pour in remainder of liquid, stir well.

8. Add liquid to pan with vegetables and stir until sauce boils and thickens.

9. Add pineapple pieces and pork and heat through. Serve with boiled rice brown rice.

# Yoghurt Chicken

Serves 4-6
Preparation time: 12 minutes
Cooking time: Convection cookery $1^1/2$ hours

## Ingredients
1 medium sized chicken
1 teaspoon salt omit salt
$^1/2$ teaspoon freshly ground black pepper
2 tablespoons lemon juice
2 cloves garlic, peeled and crushed
1 tablespoon curry powder
500 ml (1pt) natural yoghurt 500 ml (1pt) natural low-fat yoghurt
Bouquet garni (selection of fresh/dried herbs wrapped in a piece of fine muslin)
1 tablespoon butter 1 teaspoon olive oil
1 egg yolk, lightly beaten omit egg yolk
1 tablespoon flour 1 tablespoon wholemeal flour
1 tablespoon finely chopped parsley

## Method
1. Preheat oven to 180°C (350°F).
2. Prepare an ovenproof casserole dish (with lid) by spraying with cooking spray.
3. Place chicken into prepared dish.
4. Rub salt omit salt, pepper and lemon juice into chicken.
5. Stir garlic and curry powder into yoghurt. Pour over chicken.
6. Add bouquet garni.
7. Place into a moderate oven and cook for approximately $1^1/2$ hours (with lid on) until chicken is tender.
8. Remove chicken from dish and wrap in foil for 10 minutes to allow heat to distribute throughout. Reserve liquid. Skim fat off liquid and discard fat. Discard bouquet garni.
9. Remove flesh from bones. (Do not discard bones. Use to make chicken stock, see recipe page 113)
10. Add butter oil to casserole dish. Stir over a gentle heat. Remove dish from heat.
11. Add egg yolk to casserole dish omit egg yolk and mix well.
12. Place flour into a small mixing bowl. Blend with a little cold water. Stir into hot liquid in dish. Return to heat and cook until thickened, stirring constantly.
13. Return chicken pieces to liquid in dish.
14. **Convection cookery**
    Reheat at moderate temperature for approximately 10 minutes to heat through. Take care DO NOT TO BOIL mixture at this stage. or
    **Microwave cookery**
    Microwave on medium-high for approximately 3 minutes to heat through. Take care DO NOT TO BOIL mixture at this stage.
15. Garnish with parsley before serving.
    Serve with cooked vegetables, salad, rice or noodles as desired.

# The Meat*Alternative*

## Cauliflower au Gratin

Serves 4-6
Preparation time: 8 minutes
Cooking time: Convection cookery 15 minutes

### Ingredients

$^1$/$_2$ small cauliflower
2 tablespoons butter 1 tablespoon salt-reduced mono-unsaturated margarine
2 tablespoons white flour 2 tablespoons wholemeal flour
$^1$/$_2$ teaspoon salt omit salt
Freshly ground black pepper (as desired)
1 teaspoon mild English mustard
500 ml (1 pt) milk 500 ml (1 pt) low-fat milk
125 g (4 oz) grated cheddar cheese 90 g (3 oz) grated reduced-fat cheddar cheese
$^1$/$_4$ cup fresh breadcrumbs $^1$/$_4$ cup fresh wholemeal breadcrumbs
1 tablespoon Parmesan cheese

### Method

1. Break cauliflower into flowerets. Cook in a steamer until just changing colour. Take care not to overcook.
2. **Convection cookery**
   Place butter margarine into a small saucepan. Melt over a gentle heat. Remove from heat and stir in flour, salt omit salt, pepper and mustard. Return to heat and cook for 1 minute stirring constantly. Remove from heat and gradually stir in milk. Return to heat and cook over a low heat until mixture thickens, stirring constantly. or
   **Microwave cookery**
   Place butter margarine into a small microwave-safe bowl.

Microwave for 30 seconds or until butter margarine is melted. Stir in flour, salt omit salt, pepper and mustard. Microwave for 30 seconds. Gradually stir in milk. Microwave on medium-high for 1 minute and stir. Continue to microwave until mixture thickens, stirring at 1 minute intervals.
3. Stir half of the cheese into the sauce.
4. Preheat oven to 190°C (375°F).
5. Prepare a medium-sized casserole dish by spraying with cooking spray. Place cooked cauliflower into dish.
6. Pour cheese sauce over cauliflower.
7. Top with breadcrumbs, remaining cheddar cheese and Parmesan cheese.
8. Place into a moderately hot oven and bake for approximately 7 minutes or until heated through and golden brown on top.

## Cheesy Potatoes

Serves 6
Preparation time: 1 hour
Cooking time: Convection cookery 45 minutes to cook potatoes + 15 minutes to brown and heat through.
Microwave cookery 15 minutes to cook potatoes + 5 minutes to heat through.

### Ingredients

6 medium to large potatoes
1 tablespoon butter omit butter
2 tablespoons milk 2 tablespoons low-fat milk
$^1$/$_2$ teaspoon salt omit salt

Freshly ground black pepper (as desired)

I egg, lightly beaten

I cup grated cheddar cheese ³/₄ cup grated reduced-fat cheddar cheese

## Method

1. Preheat oven to 190°C (375°F).
2. Scrub potatoes. Use a skewer and prick a few holes in potatoes to prevent them bursting during cooking.
   **Convection cookery**
3. Place potatoes into an ovenproof dish and bake for approximately 45 minutes or until soft in the centre.
   **Mivrowave cookery**
   Place potatoes into a microwave safe dish. Microwave on medium high for 10 minutes or until soft in the centre.
4. When cooked, cut each potato in half. Scoop out the centre and place it into a bowl. Take care not to break through the potato skin.
5. Mash the potato. Add butter omit butter, milk, salt omit salt and pepper and mix well.
6. Pour egg into mashed potato and mix well.
7. Mix half the cheese into the mashed potato.
8. Place potato mixture back into potato cases.
9. Top with remaining cheese.
10. **Convection cookery**
    Prepare an ovenproof dish by spraying with cooking spray. Place potatoes into prepared dish and bake in a moderately hot oven for approximately
    15 minutes or until golden brown and heated through. or
    **Microwave cookery**
    Prepare a microwave-safe dish by spraying with cooking spray. Place potatoes into the prepared dish. Microwave on high for 5 minutes.

## Coleslaw

Serves 6

Preparation time: 15 minutes

Salad Dressing can be made ahead of time and added to the coleslaw just prior to serving.

## Ingredients

¹/₄ cabbage, finely shredded

3 sticks celery, cut into thin strips

I large carrot, scrubbed and grated

Salad Dressing (see recipe page 20)

## Method

1. Mix vegetables together in a large bowl. Seal until required.
2. Prior to serving pour salad dressing over coleslaw, mix well.
3. Place into a serving dish.

## Potato Salad

Serves 6

Preparation time: 8 minutes

Cooking time: Convection cookery 5 minutes

Potato can be cooked the day before and stored in an airtight container in the refrigerator.

## Ingredients

6 medium to large potatoes, peeled and cut into I cm (¹/₂ in) cubes

I onion, peeled and finely minced

¹/₃ red capsicum, finely chopped

I cup creamy mayonnaise (of your choice) use recipe for salad dressing page 20

I tablespoon Dijon mustard

2 tablespoons lemon juice

¹/₂ teaspoon salt omit salt

Freshly ground black pepper (as desired)

Pinch cayenne pepper

## Method

1. Place potato cubes into cold water in a saucepan and bring to the boil. As soon as boiling point is reached, turn off source of heat. Potato cubes must be firm and just cooked. Leave potato cubes in water for 5 minutes and strain. Potato cubes may be steamed. Spread cubes out onto a flat plate to cool. Do not make up the potato salad until cubes are completely cold. If possible cover cubes with plastic wrap and place in the refrigerator overnight.
2. Combine remaining ingredients and lightly toss through potato.

# Rice Salad

Serves 6
Preparation time: 12 minutes
Cooking time: Convection cookery 10 minutes brown rice will take longer to cook
Microwave cookery 8 minutes brown rice will take longer to cook
Rice may be cooked ahead of time and stored in a covered container in the refrigerator until required.

## Ingredients

1 cup rice 1 cup brown rice
A few strands saffron
2 cups boiling water
$^{1}/_{2}$ teaspoon salt omit salt
$^{1}/_{2}$ cup finely grated carrot
$^{1}/_{4}$ cup very finely chopped green capsicum
$^{1}/_{4}$ cup sultanas natural sultanas
1 tablespoon very finely chopped parsley
1 small onion, peeled and finely grated
2 tablespoons corn relish 2 tablespoons salt-reduced corn relish
2 tablespoons lemon juice
1 tablespoon salad oil 1 teaspoon olive oil

## Method

1. **Convection cookery**
   Place rice and saffron into a medium-sized saucepan. Pour in boiling water. Boil with lid off until rice grains are just tender. It is important not to overcook the rice or the rice salad will be spoilt. Rice can be cooked by the absorption method by just covering rice with water and allowing all the water to be absorbed by the rice during cooking. Rice can slao be cooked in a rice cooker or steamed as desired. or
   **Microwave cookery**
   Place rice and saffron into a medium-sized microwave-safe dish. Pour in boiling water. Microwave on high for 5 minutes and stir. Continue to microwave on medium high, stirring at 1 minute intervals, until rice grains are just tender. It is important not to overcook the rice or the rice salad will be spoilt. Rice can be cooked by the absorption method by just covering rice with water and allowing all the water to be absorbed by the rice during cooking Rice can be cooked in a microwave rice ccooker.

2. Rinse cooked rice in a fine colander under cold running water. If rice is cooked by the absorption method this is not necessary. Discard saffron. Spread rice out onto a flat plate to cool. If possible cover rice with plastic wrap and place in the refrigerator overnight.

3. In a large bowl, combine carrot, capsicum, sultanas, parsley and onion and toss through rice.

4. Mix corn relish, lemon juice and oil olive oil and toss through rice.

# Salmon Pâté

Serves 6-8 as an entrée
Preparation time: 20 minutes
Freshly cooked salmon can be used instead of canned salmon. It is necessary to make this pâté the day before it is required to allow it to set firmly.

## Ingredients

3 tablespoons cold water
10 g ($^{1}/_{3}$ oz) gelatine
1 x 440 g (14 oz) can pink salmon Include bones in recipe or eat seperately to add calcium to the dietary intake.
$^{1}/_{2}$ cup chopped shallots
$^{1}/_{2}$ cup dry white wine
1 teaspoon concentrated vegetable stock powder reduce stock powder to reduce salt intake
250 g (8 oz) Philadelphia™ cream cheese 180 (6 oz) Light Philadelphia™ cream cheese
Freshly ground black pepper (as desired)
1 tablespoon chopped mint
Lettuce leaves (for serving)

## Method

1. Lightly oil a medium-sized mould or basin suitable for pâté.

2. **Convection cookery**

   Place water into a small saucepan and stir in gelatine. Allow to stand for 2 minutes. Heat over a low heat to melt gelatine. Bring to the boil, taking care not to boil over. Pour into blender. or

   **Microwave cookery**

   Place water into a small microwave-safe bowl and stir in gelatine. Allow to stand for 2 minutes. Microwave on high for 1 minute. Mixture must boil, taking care not to boil over. Pour into blender.
3. Remove bones from salmon. Place salmon and liquid into the bowl of an electric blender.
4. Add remaining ingredients, expect lettuce leaves, to blender and blend until smooth.
5. Pour into prepared mould or basin.
6. Cover and refrigerate overnight.
7. To serve, remove from mould or basin onto a bed of lettuce leaves.

Salmon Paté
(see recipe opposite page)

# Spinach Pie

This lovely spinach pie can be served hot or cold. It can be served with salad or vegetables as desired.

Serves 6
Preparation time: 20 minutes
Cooking time: Convection cookery 45 minutes

## Spinach Filling

### Ingredients

6 fresh spinach leaves
**4 eggs** 3 whole eggs and 1 egg white
**1 cup milk** 1 cup low-fat milk
2 tablespoons finely chopped parsley
1 tablespoon freshly chopped basil
1 tablespoon freshly chopped dill
**1 cup grated tasty cheddar cheese** 3/4 cup grated tasty fat-reduced cheddar cheese
**Salt** omit salt
Freshly ground black pepper (as desired)
**1/2 cup grated tasty cheddar cheese (extra)** 1/3 cup grated tasty fat-reduced cheddar cheese (extra)
**2 tablespoons freshly grated Parmesan cheese** 1 tablespoon freshly grated Parmesan cheese

### Method

1. Wash and finely chop spinach leaves.
2. Place leaves into a steamer and lightly steam, with lid on.
3. Place leaves into a medium-sized mixing bowl.
4. Break eggs into a small bowl and lightly beat. Add milk, herbs, cheese, salt omit salt and pepper and mix well. Pour into bowl with spinach and mix well.

## Pastry

### Ingredients

**2 cups white flour** 1 cup white flour and 1 cup wholemeal flour
**1/2 teaspoon baking powder**
**100 g (3 1/2 oz) butter** 90 g (3 oz) salt-reduced mono-unsaturated margarine

100 ml (3½ oz) water
1 teaspoon lemon juice
1 egg yolk omit egg yolk

**Method**

1. Preheat oven to 180°C (350°F).
2. Prepare a 25 cm (10 in) flat pie dish by spraying with cooking spray.
3. Sift white flour and baking powder into a medium-sized mixing bowl. Stir in wholemeal flour. Rub butter margarine into dry ingredients with the tips of the fingers until mixture resembles fine breadcrumbs. This process may be done using an electric food processor.
4. Pour water into a small basin. Add lemon juice and egg yolk omit egg yolk and mix well. Pour liquid into dry ingredients. When substituting wholemeal flour, it may be necessary to add a little more water to sufficiently moisten mixture. Mixture should be a firm consistency.
5. Turn dough out onto a lightly floured board and knead lightly. Roll dough out to 0.5 cm (¼ in) thickness.
6. Line base of pie dish with pastry. Any remaining pastry can be kept and used to decorate top of pie.
7. Pour filling into prepared pastry case.
8. Decorate top of pie with any remaining pastry.
9. Sprinkle extra cheddar cheese and Parmesan cheese over pie.
10. Place pie into a moderate oven and cook for approximately 45 minutes or until set in the centre when tested.

An alternative to making your own pastry is to use filo pastry. Filo pastry has no added fat. Make up the spinach filling according to the recipe above. Use small portions of filling and wrap in filo pastry. Reduce the baking time for smaller portions.

# Stuffed Pumpkin

Serves 12-16 depending on size of pumpkin
Preparation time: 12 minutes
Cooking time: Convection cookery 2-3 hours
Microwave cookery 30 minutes

## Ingredients

1 medium-sized pumpkin, with stalk attached (The size depends on the number to be served. A medium-sized pumpkin will serve 12-16.)

## Seasoning

### Ingredients

2 medium-sized tomatoes
Boiling water
2 tablespoons butter omit butter
3 rashers bacon, finely chopped all fat and rind removed
3 shallots, finely chopped
1 teaspoon lemon rind
1 tablespoon lemon juice
Fresh herbs (as desired, or ½ teaspoon mixed dried herbs)
½ to ¾ loaf (depending on size of pumpkin) white bread wholemeal bread, made into breadcrumbs
1 tablespoon rice bran to increase fibre in the diet
Salt omit salt
Freshly ground black pepper (as desired)
1 tablespoon chopped parsley
300 ml (½ pt) sour cream 200 ml (7 fl oz) lite sour cream

### Method

1. Preheat oven to 180°C (350°F).
2. Prepare a large (Pyrex®) casserole dish by spraying with cooking spray.
3. Mark a circle on the centre top of the pumpkin with a saucer. Cut circle area at a slight angle to stalk. This becomes the lid of the pumpkin. Scoop pumpkin seeds out with a metal spoon.
4. Place tomatoes into a small basin. Cover with boiling water. Allow to stand for 2 minutes. Remove skins and

chop tomatoes. Place into a large mixing bowl.

5. Add remaining ingredients omit butter and salt, except sour cream, to bowl and mix well.

6. Fill cavity in pumpkin with seasoning. Replace lid on pumpkin.

7. Place pumpkin into prepared casserole dish.

8. **Convection cookery**

   Place into a moderate oven and bake for 2-3 hours or until pumpkin is soft when tested. or

**Microwave cookery**

Microwave on high for 15 minutes. Continue to microwave on medium-high for a further
15 minutes or until pumpkin is cooked when tested.

9. Remove lid from pumpkin and carefully stir sour cream into stuffing. Replace and allow to stand for 10 minutes before serving.

   Can be served hot or cold.

Stuffed Pumpkin

(see recipe opposite page)

## Tabouli

Serves 4-6
Preparation time: 10 minutes + 1 hour to soak cracked wheat.
Wheat can be soaked ahead of time. This recipe is best when
chilled for several hours before serving.

### Ingredients

1 cup cracked wheat
2 cups cold water
1/2 cup finely chopped parsley
1/4 cup finely chopped mint
1 cup finely chopped shallots
2 firm tomatoes, cut into 1 cm (1/2in) cubes
2 tablespoons olive oil  1 tablespoon olive oil
2 tablespoons lemon juice  1 tablespoon lemon juice as desired
Salt  omit salt
Freshly ground black pepper (as desired)

### Method

1. Place cracked wheat into a medium-sized bowl. Pour in cold
water. Allow to stand for 1 hour.
2. Strain cracked wheat and squeeze out and discard excess liquid. Place wheat into a medium-sized bowl.
3. Mix remaining ingredients through cracked wheat.
4. Chill for several hours before serving.

## Tuna Casserole

Serves 6
Preparation time: 20 minutes
Cooking time: Convection cookery 10 minutes  Brown rice will
take longer to cook
Microwave cookery 5 minutes  Brown rice will take longer to
cook
Rice may be cooked ahead of time and stored in a covered
container in the refrigerator until required.

### Ingredients

1 1/4 cups white rice  1 1/4 cups brown rice
3 cups cold water
2 1/2 cups cornflakes
60 g (2 oz) butter  30 g (1 oz) salt-reduced mono-unsaturated
margarine or 1 tablespoon olive oil
1 x 400 g (14 oz) can tuna  no oil, no added salt
1 cup frozen peas
1 large onion, peeled and finely chopped
1 x 400 g (14 oz) can peeled tomatoes  no added salt, drain
tomatoes and discard liquid or reserve for stock
1 1/2 cups milk  1 1/2 cups low-fat milk (approximately)
2 tablespoons cornflour
2 tablespoons butter  1 tablespoon salt-reduced mono-unsaturated
margarine or 1 tablespoon olive oil
2 tablespoons finely chopped fresh parsley
1/4 teaspoon dried basil leaves
1/2 teaspoon salt  omit salt
Freshly ground black pepper (as desired)
1/2 cup grated cheddar cheese  1/3 cup reduced-fat cheddar cheese
2 tablespoons freshly grated Parmesan cheese  1 tablespoon freshly
grated Parmesan cheese
sprigs of fresh parsley (for garnish)

### Method

1. **Convection cookery**
   Place rice and water into a large saucepan. Cook with lid off
   over a low heat until rice is tender and water is absorbed.
   Rice can be cooked in a rice cooker or steamer as desired.
   Strain rice, cover and set aside. or
   **Microwave cookery**
   Place rice and water into a medium-sized microwave-safe
   bowl. Microwave on high for 7 minutes or until rice is tender and water is absorbed. Cover rice and set aside. Rice can
   be cooked in a microwave rice cooker.
2. Prepare a 2-litre (Pyrex®) casserole dish by spraying with
   cooking spray.
3. **Convection cookery**
   Preheat oven to 180°C (350°F).
4. Place cornflakes into a medium-sized mixing bowl and

Tabouli (see recipe opposite page)

lightly crush.

5. **Convection cookery**

   Place 60 g (2 oz) butter 30 g (1 oz) margarine into a small saucepan and melt over a gentle heat. Pour butter margarine or oil over cornflakes in mixing bowl and mix well. or

   **Microwave cookery**

   Place 60 g (2 oz) butter 30 g (1 oz) margarine into a medium-sized microwave-safe bowl. Cover and microwave on high for 40 seconds or until butter margarine is melted. Pour butter margarine or oil over cornflakes in mixing bowl and mix well.

6. Place half the cornflake mixture into the bottom of prepared casserole dish.

7. Spread 1 cup cooked rice over cornflake mixture.

8. Drain tuna and reserve liquid. Spread tuna over rice in casserole dish.

9. Spread peas over tuna in casserole dish.

10. **Convection cookery**

    Lightly spray a non-stick frying pan with cooking spray. Lightly cook onion and place into casserole dish. or

    **Microwave cookery**

    Place onion into a small microwave-safe bowl. Cover and microwave on high for 1 minute. Place into casserole dish.

11. Chop tomatoes and spread over ingredients in casserole dish.

12. Pour reserved tuna liquid into a measuring jug. Add milk to make 2 cups of liquid.

13. Place cornflour into a small bowl. Add a little tuna liquid and blend well. Gradually stir in remaining liquid.

14. Convection cookery Melt 2 tablespoons butter 1 tablespoon margarine in a medium-sized saucepan. Stir butter margarine or oil into liquid. Pour liquid into saucepan and cook over a low heat, stirring until sauce boils and thickens. or

    **Microwave cookery**

    Place 2 tablespoons butter 1 tablespoon margarine into a medium-sized microwave-safe mixing bowl. Cover and microwave on high for 40 seconds or until butter margarine melts. Pour butter margarine or oil into bowl and stir. Microwave on high for 1 minute and stir. Continue to microwave on high, stirring at 40-second intervals, until sauce thickens.

15. Stir parsley, basil, salt omit salt, and black pepper into sauce.

16. Pour sauce over casserole.

17. Top with remaining rice.

18. Sprinkle with cheeses and remaining cornflake mixture.

19. Convection cookery Place into a moderate oven and bake for approximately 10 minutes or until heated through. or

    **Microwave cookery**

    Microwave on high for approximately 5 minutes or until heated through.

20. Garnish with sprigs of fresh parsley.

# Luncheon*Ideas*

## Fried Rice

Serves 4-6
Preparation time: 10 minutes
Cooking time: Convection cookery 30 minutes brown rice will take longer to cook

### Ingredients

3 tablespoons butter 2 teaspoons olive oil and 1 teaspoon sesame oil
1 cup white rice 1 cup brown rice
1 packet chicken noodle soup mix salt-reduced chicken noodle soup mix
3 cups hot water
$^{1}/_{2}$ cup finely diced celery
1 cup finely chopped shallots
$^{1}/_{2}$ cup diced red capsicum
$^{1}/_{2}$ cup diced green capsicum
3 rashers bacon, cut into small pieces all fat and rind removed
3 eggs eggs can be omitted or use 2 whole eggs and 1 egg white
$^{1}/_{2}$ teaspoon salt omit salt
Freshly ground black pepper (as desired)

### Method

1. Heat an electric frypan to 170°C (340°F). (Point no. 7 on a dial of 1-10.)
2. Place butter oil into frypan.
3. Place rice into frypan and stir continuously until rice is a golden colour. If using brown rice, take care not to burn rice.
4. Add soup mix and water to pan.
5. Simmer uncovered until all the liquid is absorbed. Stir frequently to prevent rice sticking to frypan.
6. Add celery, shallots and capsicum to rice in frypan.
7. Place lid on pan and turn off.
8. **Convection cookery**
   Place bacon into a frying pan and lightly fry. Add bacon to rice in frypan. Bacon can be grilled. or
   **Microwave cookery**
   Place bacon onto paper towel on a flat microwave-safe plate. Cover with paper towel. Microwave on high for 1 minute. Turn bacon and microwave for a further 1 minute. Add bacon to rice in frypan.
9. **Convection cookery**
   Place eggs into a medium-sized bowl. Lightly beat. Pour into frying pan. Cook over a gentle heat. When set, cut into thin strips and add to rice in pan. or
   **Microwave cookery**
   Place eggs into a medium-sized bowl and lightly beat. Pour onto a flat microwave-safe plate. Microwave on medium-high for 40 seconds or until egg is set. When cooked, cut into thin strips and add to rice in pan.
10. Season with salt omit salt and pepper as desired.
11. Reheat before serving, stirring occasionally to prevent rice sticking to frypan.

## Salmon Quiche

This recipe will suit the cook who wants a good quality finished product with a minimum of effort.

Serves 4-6
Preparation time: 7 minutes
Cooking time: Convection cookery 30 minutes
Microwave cookery 12 minutes

### Ingredients

250 g (8 oz) lean bacon all fat and rind removed
1 large onion, peeled and finely chopped
2 teaspoons finely chopped parsley
1¼ cups breadcrumbs 1¼ cups wholemeal breadcrumbs
1 cup grated cheddar cheese ¾ cup grated reduced-fat cheddar cheese
Freshly ground black pepper (as desired)
1 cup milk 1 cup low-fat milk (warmed)
¼ cup sour cream ⅓ cup light sour cream
3 eggs, lightly beaten use 2 whole eggs and 1 egg white
1 teaspoon mild English mustard
1 x 440 g (14 oz) can pink salmon. Include bones in recipe or eat separately to add calcium to the dietary intake.

### Method

1. Preheat oven to180°C (350°F).
2. Prepare a quiche dish by spraying with cooking spray.
3. Chop bacon into small pieces. Place into prepared quiche dish.
4. Place remaining ingredients into a medium-sized mixing bowl and mix to combine. Pour over bacon.
5. **Convection cookery**
   Place into a moderate oven and bake for approximately 30 minutes or until cooked when tested. or
   **Microwave cookery**
   Microwave on medium-high for approximately 12 minutes or until cooked when tested. Allow to stand for 5 minutes before serving.

## Stuffed Tomatoes

Makes 12
Preparation time: 12 minutes
Cooking time: Convection cookery 2 hours
Microwave cookery 20 minutes

### Ingredients

12 large tomatoes
½ cup tomato paste no added salt
1 teaspoon salt omit salt
Freshly ground black pepper (as desired)
4 tablespoons olive oil 2 tablespoons olive oil
1 onion, peeled and finely chopped
2 cloves garlic, peeled and finely chopped
600 g (1¼ lb) finely ground minced meat lean minced steak
1 tablespoon finely chopped parsley
125 g (4 oz) vermicelli pasta, broken up very finely
1 tablespoon rice bran to increase fibre in the diet

### Method

1. Preheat oven to 150°C (300°F).
2. Prepare a 33 cm x 23 cm (13 in x 9 in) casserole dish by spraying with cooking spray.
3. Slice 1 cm (½ in) off the top of each tomato.
4. **Convection cookery**
   Carefully scoop pulp out of tomatoes. Chop pulp and place in a medium-sized saucepan. Add tomato paste. Simmer with lid on for 20 minutes. Rub through a fine sieve. Reserve liquid and discard pulp. or
   **Microwave cookery**
   Carefully scoop pulp out of tomatoes. Chop pulp and place into a medium-sized microwave-safe bowl. Add tomato paste. Cover with plastic wrap and microwave on high for 5 minutes and stir. Microwave on high for a further 3 minutes. Rub through a fine sieve. Reserve liquid and discard pulp.
5. Sprinkle tomato cases with a little salt omit salt and pepper (as desired).
6. Pour 1 tablespoon 1 teaspoon olive oil into a large frying pan. Add onion and garlic and sauté (lightly fry).

7. Pour tomato liquid into a large bowl. Add minced meat, onion, garlic, salt omit salt and pepper, parsley and vermicelli and rice bran and mix well.

8. Fill tomato cases with meat mixture and replace the tomato tops.

9. **Convection cookery**
   Place into prepared dish and spoon a little of the remaining olive oil over tomatoes. Lightly brush tomatoes with oil. Place into a slow oven and bake for approximately 1$\frac{1}{2}$ hours or until vermicelli is soft. or

**Microwave cookery**
Place into prepared dish and spoon a little of the remaining olive oil over tomatoes. Lightly brush tomatoes with oil. Microwave on medium-high for approximately 20 minutes or until vermicelli is soft.

Serve hot or cold, as an entrée, luncheon dish or as an accompaniment to a main meal.

Spinach Pie (see recipe page 53)
Stuffed Tomatoes (see recipe page 60)

# Desserts *Desserts*

## Apple Crumble

Serves 4-6
Preparation time: 12 minutes
Cooking time: Convection cookery 6 minutes to cook apple
+ 15 minutes baking time
Apple may be cooked ahead of time and stored in a covered
container in the refrigerator until required.

### Ingredients

3 large green cooking apples
$^1/_2$ cup water
$^1/_3$ cup sugar  $^1/_4$ cup sugar
$^1/_4$ cup white self-raising flour  $^1/_4$ cup wholemeal self-raising flour
2 tablespoons butter  I tablespoon salt-reduced mono-unsaturated
margarine
2 tablespoons brown sugar
$^1/_2$ teaspoon vanilla essence
2 tablespoons almond flakes
I tablespoon caster sugar

### Method

1. Preheat oven to 180°C (350°F).
2. Prepare a 2 litre (4 pt) (Pyrex®) casserole dish by spraying
   with cooking spray.
3. Peel and core apples and chop into small dice.
4. **Convection cookery**
   Place apple into a medium-sized saucepan. Pour in water
   and stir in sugar. Cook with lid on over a low heat until
   apple is soft. Strain and discard liquid and place apple into
   prepared casserole dish. or

Microwave cookery
Place apple into prepared casserole dish. Pour in water and
stir in sugar. Cover and microwave on high for 4 minutes or
until apple is soft. Strain and discard liquid and leave apple
in dish.
5. Sift white flour into a medium-sized mixing bowl. Stir in
   wholemeal flour. Rub butter margarine into dry ingredients
   with the tips of the fingers until mixture resembles fine
   breadcrumbs. This process may be done using an electric
   food processor. Stir in brown sugar and vanilla. Sprinkle
   crumble mixture over apple.
6. Mix almond flakes and caster sugar. Sprinkle over crumble
   mixture.
7. Place into a moderate oven and bake for approximately
   15 minutes or until golden brown and pastry is cooked.
   Serve with custard (see recipe page 69)

## Apple Strudel

Serves 6
Preparation time: 20 minutes
Cooking time: Convection cookery 20 minutes

### Ingredients

6 cooking apples
$^1/_2$ cup water
2 tablespoons sugar  I tablespoon sugar
12 whole cloves
2 tablespoons sultanas  natural sultanas
2 teaspoons finely grated lemon rind
2 x 25 cm x 25 cm (10 in x 10 in) sheets prepared frozen puff

pastry Strudel is traditionally made using puff pastry, however filo pastry contains no added fat and can be substituted

1 egg white, lightly beaten (for glazing)
2 tablespoons caster sugar 1 tablespoon caster sugar
60 g (2 oz) almond flakes

## Method

1. Preheat oven to 200°C (400°F).
2. Prepare a flat oven tray by spraying with cooking spray.
3. Peel and core apples and cut into small dice.
4. **Convection cookery**
   Place apple into a medium-sized saucepan. Pour in water and add sugar and cloves. Cook, with lid on, over a low heat until apple is soft. Reduce heat and cook gently for 5 minutes or until apple is soft. Strain and discard liquid and cloves. or
   **Microwave cookery**
   Place apple into a medium-sized microwave-safe bowl. Pour in water and add sugar and cloves. Cover and microwave on high for 3 minutes or until apple is soft. Strain and discard liquid and cloves.
5. Stir in sultanas and lemon rind.
6. Using one sheet of puff pastry, place half the mixture about one third of the way from the edge. Use about 6 thicknesses of filo pastry. Lightly brush between each sheet with canola oil or brush with cooking spray. Roll pastry over mixture. Place roll onto prepared tray. Make a few deep cuts on top of pastry with a sharp knife. Repeat with remaining mixture and other sheet of puff pastry. Repeat with remaining mixture and another 6 sheets of filo pastry.
7. Glaze pastry with egg white. Sprinkle with caster sugar and almond flakes.
8. Place into a moderately hot oven and bake for approximately 20 minutes or until golden brown and pastry is cooked.

   Serve hot or cold with custard (see recipe page 69), cream omit cream or icecream reduced-fat icecream as desired. Strudel is best eaten the day it is made.

# Blanc Mange

This was a very popular dessert at one time. It is now seldom served, as it is considered not 'fancy' enough for today's style of cuisine. This is a shame as it is a nutritious dessert that is low in fat.

Serves 2
Preparation time: 5 minutes
Cooking time: Convection cookery 5 minutes
Microwave cookery 3 minutes

## Ingredients

3 tablespoons arrowroot or cornflour
2 tablespoons sugar 1 tablespoon sugar
2 cups milk 2 cups low-fat milk

## Method

1. **Convection cookery**
   Place arrowroot and sugar into a medium-sized saucepan. Blend with a little of the milk. Stir in remaining milk. Bring to the boil and cook, stirring constantly until mixture thickens. or
   **Microwave cookery**
   Place arrowroot and sugar into a medium-sized microwave-safe bowl. Blend with a little of the milk. Stir in remaining milk. Microwave on high for 1 minute and stir. Continue to microwave on medium-high, stirring at 1-minute intervals until mixture boils and thickens.
2. Pour into a serving bowl and allow to set before serving.

# Chocolate Blanc Mange

Serves 2
Preparation time: 5 minutes
Cooking time: Convection cookery 5 minutes
Microwave cookery 3 minutes

## Ingredients

3 tablespoons arrowroot or cornflour
1 tablespoon cocoa
2 tablespoons sugar 1 tablespoon sugar
2 cups milk 2 cups low-fat milk

## Method

1. **Convection cookery**

   Place arrowroot, cocoa and sugar into a medium-sized saucepan. Blend with a little of the milk. Stir in remaining milk. Bring to the boil and cook, stirring constantly until mixture thickens. or

   **Microwave cookery**

   Place arrowroot, cocoa and sugar into a medium-sized microwave-safe bowl. Blend with a little of the milk. Stir in remaining milk. Microwave on high for 1 minute and stir. Continue to microwave on medium-high, stirring at 1 minute intervals until mixture boils and thickens.

2. Pour into a serving bowl and allow to set before serving.

## Bread and Butter Custard

This is a very delicious dessert that is not used a great deal these days. It was originally designed as a way of using up stale bread.

Serves 6
Preparation time: 15 minutes
Cooking time: Convection cookery 40 minutes

### Ingredients

¹/₄ cup sultanas natural sultanas
2 teaspoons butter omit butter
2 teaspoons raspberry jam
2 slices bread 2 slices wholemeal bread
2 eggs
2 tablespoons sugar
600 ml (1 pt) milk 600 ml (1 pt) low-fat milk
¹/₂ teaspoon vanilla essence
2 teaspoons coconut omit coconut
Ground nutmeg (to sprinkle on top)

### Method

1. Preheat oven to 150°C (300°F).
2. Prepare a 2 litre (4 pt) ovenproof pie dish by spraying with cooking spray.
3. Sprinkle sultanas into bottom of prepared dish.
4. Spread butter omit butter and jam over bread.
5. Cut bread into fingers and place over sultanas in dish.
6. Place eggs into a medium-sized mixing bowl. Add sugar and beat well. Stir in milk and vanilla. Pour over bread.
7. Sprinkle with coconut omit coconut and nutmeg.
8. Place pie dish into a larger ovenproof dish. Pour in enough cold water to go about half way up the pie dish.
9. Place into a moderate oven and bake for approximately 40 minutes or until custard is set in the centre when tested with the point of a sharp-bladed knife. When cooked, carefully remove from oven.
10. Remove custard from baking dish of hot water, allow to cool.

## Butterscotch Sponge

Serves 4-6
Preparation time: 15 minutes
Cooking time: Convection cookery 8 minutes
Microwave cookery 5 minutes

### Ingredients

¹/₂ cup butter ¹/₄ cup salt-reduced mono-unsaturated margarine
1 cup brown sugar ³/₄ cup brown sugar
3 eggs
2 cups milk 2 cups low-fat milk
1 tablespoon gelatine
¹/₄ cup cold water

### Method

1. **Convection cookery**

   Place butter margarine into a small saucepan and melt over a gentle heat. Remove from heat and add brown sugar. Return to heat and stir continuously over heat for 1 minute. or

   **Microwave cookery**

   Place butter margarine into a small microwave-safe bowl. Cover and microwave on high for 40 seconds or until butter margarine is melted. Stir in brown sugar. Microwave on high for 1 minute.

Blanc Mange (see recipe page 63)

Bread and Butter Custard (see recipe opposite page)

2. Separate eggs and place yolks into a small basin. Place whites into a separate medium-sized clean, dry bowl.

3. Convection cookery Pour milk into a small saucepan and warm over a gentle heat. DO NOT BOIL. or
   **Microwave cookery**
   Pour milk into a small microwave-safe bowl. Microwave on high for 1 minute or until milk is hot. DO NOT BOIL.

4. Add milk to yolks and mix well. Stir into butter margarine and brown sugar.

5. **Convection cookery**
   Cook over a gentle heat until mixture is the consistency of a smooth custard. DO NOT BOIL. or Microwave cookery Microwave on high for 1 minute and stir. Continue to microwave on medium-low until mixture is the consistency of a smooth custard. DO NOT BOIL.

6. Remove from heat and allow to cool. It is important to cool the custard or it will curdle when the egg whites are added.

7. Place gelatine into a small bowl. Stir in cold water and allow to stand for 5 minutes.

8. **Convection cookery**
   Pour gelatine and water into a small saucepan and heat over a gentle heat until just boiling. Take care not to boil over. Remove from heat and allow to cool slightly. Stir into cooled custard mixture. or
   **Microwave cookery**
   Pour gelatine and water into a small microwave-safe bowl. Microwave on high for 40 seconds. Take care not to boil over. Allow to cool slightly. Stir into cooled custard mixture.

9. Beat egg whites until stiff. Fold into cooled custard mixture.

10. Pour into a dish or mould. Refrigerate until set.
    Serve with custard (see recipe page 69) and/or fruit as desired.

# Chocolate Mousse

My younger daughter asked me to include this recipe. It was a family favourite as she grew up in our home.

Makes 6 small individual serves
Preparation time: 12 minutes (It will take at least 4 hours to set before it is ready to serve.)

**Ingredients**

1 x 375 ml can evaporated milk 1 x 375 ml can low-fat evaporated milk

3 eggs 2 whole eggs and 1 egg white, separated

2 tablespoons cocoa

3 tablespoons sugar 2 tablespoons sugar

1 tablespoon gelatine

$^1/_4$ cup cold water

$^1/_2$ cup cream $^1/_4$ cup lite cream

$^1/_2$ teaspoon vanilla essence

**Method**

1. **Convection cookery**
   Combine evaporated milk, egg yolks, cocoa and sugar in a small saucepan. Whisk with a beater. Place gelatine into a small bowl. Pour in warm water and allow to dissolve. Pour into saucepan. Stir over a low heat until mixture is hot. DO NOT BOIL. or
   **Microwave cookery**
   Combine evaporated milk, egg yolks, cocoa and sugar in a small microwave-safe bowl. Whisk with a beater. Place gelatine into a separate small bowl. Pour in cold water and allow to dissolve. Pour into microwave-safe bowl. Microwave on high for 30 seconds and stir. Microwave on medium for a further minute. DO NOT BOIL.

2. Allow mixture to cool.

3. Pour cream into a small mixing bowl. Pour in vanilla. Whip cream. Lightly fold into cooled chocolate mixture.

4. In a separate, clean, dry bowl, beat egg whites until stiff. Lightly stir into chocolate mixture.

5. Refrigerate until just starting to set. This will take approximately 1 hour.

6. Gently stir to evenly mix egg whites throughout mixture.
7. Pour into individual serving bowls.
8. Refrigerate until required. Note that it will need at least 4 hours to set.

## Chocolate Sauce Pudding

Serves 4-6
Preparation time: 15 minutes
Cooking time: Convection cookery 20 minutes
Microwave cookery 8 minutes

### Ingredients

I cup white self-raising flour I cup wholemeal self-raising flour
2 tablespoons cocoa
$^2/_3$ cup caster sugar $^1/_2$ cup caster sugar
$^3/_4$ cup milk $^3/_4$ cup low-fat milk
I teaspoon vanilla essence
60 g (2 oz) butter 40 g (1$^1/_2$ oz) salt-reduced mono-unsaturated margarine
I tablespoon cocoa (extra)
$^1/_3$ cup brown sugar $^1/_4$ cup brown sugar
1$^1/_4$ cups fresh black coffee (for best flavour use fresh, strongly brewed coffee or use 1$^1/_2$ teaspoons instant coffee in boiling water)

### Method

1. Preheat oven to 180°C (350°F).
2. Prepare a medium-sized casserole dish by spraying with cooking spray.
3. Sift white flour and cocoa into a medium-sized mixing bowl. Stir in wholemeal flour. Stir in sugar.
4. Pour in milk and vanilla and stir.
5. Stir in butter margarine. (Butter or margarine must be very soft. It can be softened in the microwave if necessary.)
6. Beat for 2 minutes using a hand-held electric mixer until ingredients are well combined. (Beat with a wooden spoon if an electric mixer is not available.) When substituting wholemeal flour, it may be necessary to add a little more milk to moisten cake mixture. Cake mixture should be a moist consistency.
7. Pour into prepared dish.

8. Place the extra 1 tablespoon cocoa into a small mixing bowl. Stir in brown sugar. Sprinkle over mixture.
9. Carefully pour hot coffee over mixture.
10. **Convection cookery**
    Place into a moderate oven and cook for approximately 20 minutes or until cake mixture is cooked when tested. or
    **Microwave cookery**
    Microwave on high for approximately 8 minutes or until cake mixture is cooked when tested.
11. Allow to stand for 5 minutes before serving.
    Delicious served hot or cold with cream omit cream, icecream reduced-fat icecream or custard (see recipe page 69) as desired.

## Creamed Rice

Serves 6
Preparation time: 5 minutes
Cooking time:  Convection cookery 30 minutes brown rice will take longer to cook
Microwave cookery 10 minutes brown rice will take longer to cook

### Ingredients

I cup warm water
$^1/_2$ cup white rice $^1/_2$ cup brown rice
4 cups milk 4 cups low-fat milk
I thin strip orange rind
3 egg yolks 2 egg yolks
I tablespoon cornflour 2 tablespoons cornflour
$^1/_3$ cup sugar $^1/_4$ cup sugar
I teaspoon vanilla essence
Ground nutmeg or cinnamon (to sprinkle on top)

### Method

1. **Convection cookery**
   Place water and rice into a large saucepan. Stir over a medium heat until water is absorbed. or
   **Microwave cookery**
   Place water and rice into a large microwave-safe bowl. Microwave on high for 5 minutes and stir. Continue to

microwave until water is absorbed.

2. Remove from heat. Add milk and stir well. Add strip of orange rind.

3. **Convection cookery**
Return to heat and bring to the boil. Reduce heat and simmer gently for approximately 20 minutes or until rice is soft. Stir frequently to prevent rice sticking to the bottom of the saucepan. Remove from heat. or
**Microwave cookery**
Microwave on medium until rice is soft, stirring occasionally.

4. Place egg yolks into a small bowl. Stir in cornflour and sugar. Add a little extra cold milk and mix well. Take $1/2$ cup hot liquid from rice and slowly stir into egg yolk mixture.

5. **Convection cookery**
Return egg yolk mixture to saucepan and mix well. Stir over a gentle heat until mixture thickens. DO NOT BOIL. or
**Microwave cookery**
Return egg yolk mixture to microwave-safe bowl and mix well. Microwave on medium for 1 minute and stir. Continue to microwave for 1 minute intervals until mixture thickens. DO NOT BOIL.

6. Remove strip of orange rind.

7. Stir in vanilla.

8. Pour into a serving dish. Sprinkle with nutmeg or cinnamon.
Serve hot or cold with fruit as desired.

## Christmas Pudding

Serves 20
Preparation time: 30 minutes
Cooking time: Convection cookery 5 hours for 1 large pudding
($3^1/2$ hours each for 2 smaller puddings)
The best flavour is obtained if fruits are soaked in rum overnight.

### Ingredients
**500 g (1 lb) raisins** natural raisins
**500 g (1 lb) sultanas** natural sultanas
**125 g (4 oz) dates, chopped**
**125 g (4 oz) glace cherries** 100 g (3 oz) glace cherries **(chopped)**
**125 g (4 oz) mixed peel**
**125 ml (4 fl oz) rum**
**500 g (1 lb) butter** 400 g (14 oz) salt-reduced mono-unsaturated margarine
**500 g (1 lb) brown sugar** 400 g (14 oz) brown sugar
**10 eggs** 8 eggs
**6 small-medium carrots, peeled and finely grated**
**2 cooking apples, peeled and grated**
**2 tablespoons treacle**
**125 g (4 oz) chopped blanched almonds**
**500 g (1 lb) fine white breadcrumbs** 500 g (1 lb) fine wholemeal breadcrumbs
**125 g (4 oz) white flour** 125 g (4 oz) wholemeal flour
**1 teaspoon mixed spice**
**$1/2$ teaspoon cinnamon**
**$1/4$ teaspoon nutmeg**
**$1/2$ teaspoon salt** omit salt
**Extra rum to pour over cooked pudding(s) (2 tablespoons for each pudding)**

### Method
1. Place fruits and peel into a large container. Pour in rum. Seal container and leave overnight.

2. Prepare one large or two smaller pudding steamer(s) with tight fitting lid(s) by spraying with cooking spray.

3. Next day, cream butter margarine and sugar.

4. Add eggs one at a time beating well after each addition.

5. Place creamed mixture into a large mixing bowl. Stir in soaked fruits and peel, carrot, apple, treacle, almonds and breadcrumbs.

6. Sift white flour, spices and salt omit salt into fruit mixture. Stir in wholemeal flour. When substituting wholemeal flour, it may be necessary to add a little milk to sufficiently moisten mixture. Mixture should be a very moist consistency.

7. Place mixture into prepared steamer(s). Secure lid(s). Place into saucepan.

8. Half-fill saucepan(s) with cold water and bring to the boil.

9. Steam one pudding for approximately 5 hours or two

smaller puddings for $3^1/_2$ hours each, with lid on saucepan. Water must boil gently during cooking. It may be necessary to add a little more boiling water during cooking.

10. When cooked, remove steamer(s) from saucepan(s).
11. Pour extra rum over pudding(s).
12. Allow pudding(s) to cool in steamer(s).

When required for serving, re-steam for 2 hours for 1 large pudding or 1 hour each for smaller puddings. Serve with Brandy Sauce (Hard Sauce) (see recipe below) or custard (see recipe on page 69) Use brandy sauce (hard sauce) sparingly, but it is Christmas so allow yourself a little. Individual slices of pudding can be heated in the microwave oven. Allow approximately 1 minute per slice for heating. This is a very effective and convenient way of reheating.

## Brandy Sauce (Hard Sauce)

Makes 1 x 300 ml (10 oz) jar
Preparation time: 5 minutes

### Ingredients

125 g (4 oz) unsalted butter 90 g (3 oz) salt-reduced mon-ounsaturated margarine

2 cups icing sugar mixture, sifted 1³/₄ cups icing sugar mixture

2 tablespoons brandy

$^1/_2$ teaspoon vanilla essence

### Method

1. Place butter margarine into a small bowl. Gradually add icing sugar, beating well after each addition.
2. Stir in brandy and vanilla.
3. Store in a screw top jar in the refrigerator until required.

Serve small portions with Christmas pudding.

## Custard

Serves 4-6
Preparation time: 5 minutes
Cooking time: Convection cookery 7 minutes
Microwave cookery 5 minutes

### Ingredients

2 tablespoons cornflour

600 ml (1 pt) milk 600 ml (1 pt) low-fat milk

1 egg, lightly beaten

2 tablespoons cream omit cream

3 tablespoons sugar 2 tablespoons sugar

$^1/_2$ teaspoon vanilla essence

### Method

1. Place cornflour into a small bowl. Blend with a little of the milk. Stir in remainder of the milk.
2. Add egg and cream omit cream and whisk well.
3. **Convection cookery**
   Pour into a small saucepan. Stir constantly over a low heat until custard thickens. DO NOT BOIL or custard may curdle. or
   **Microwave cookery**
   Pour into a small microwave-safe bowl. Microwave on medium for 1 minute and stir. Continue to microwave on medium-low, stirring at 1-minute intervals until custard thickens. DO NOT BOIL or custard may curdle.
4. Stir in sugar and vanilla.

## Custard Tart

This is a quick-mix recipe. It is very easy to prepare. It can be cooked in a foil tray and easily transported. The tart will have a firm base representing a pastry base. It is best made the day before it is required. It is not suitable for freezing. When the recipe is made using potato flour instead of white flour, it is then suitable to serve on a gluten-free diet.

Serves 6
Preparation time: 5 minutes
Cooking time: Convection cookery 35 minutes
Microwave cookery 10 minutes

### Ingredients

1 tablespoon butter 1 teaspoon salt-reduced mono-unsaturated margarine (softened)

1/2 cup brown sugar 1/3 cup brown sugar

1 tablespoon plain flour 1 tablespoon potato flour

125 g (4 oz) Philadelphia™ cream cheese 90 g (3 oz) Light Philadelphia™ cream cheese

3 eggs 2 whole eggs and 1 egg white

2 cups milk 2 cups low-fat milk

1/2 teaspoon vanilla essence

Nutmeg (to sprinkle on top)

### Method

1. Preheat oven to 160°C (325°F) for convection cookery.
2. Prepare a 23 cm (9 in) round pie dish by spraying with cooking spray.
3. Place all the ingredients, expect nutmeg, into a blender use potato flour, for a gluten-free diet, instead of white flour. Blend until smooth. (Ingredients can be beaten well using a hand-held mixer, or beaten with a wooden spoon.)
4. Pour into prepared dish.
5. Place dish into a larger ovenproof dish. Pour in enough cold water to go about halfway up the pie dish.
6. Sprinkle top of custard tart with nutmeg.
7. **Convection cookery**
   Place into a moderately slow oven and bake for approximately 35 minutes or until custard is set in the centre when tested with the point of a sharp knife. When cooked, care-

fully remove from oven. Remove tart from dish of hot water and allow to cool. or

   **Microwave cookery**
   Microwave on medium high for approximately 10 minutes or until custard is set in the centre when tested with the point of a sharp knife. When tart is cooked, carefully remove from dish of hot water and allow to cool.
8. Refrigerate before serving.
   Serve with whipped cream omit cream, icecream reduced-fat icecream or custard (see recipe page 69) as desired.

## Golden Syrup Dumplings

Dumplings are traditionally cooked on the stove top. This recipe is cooked in the microwave oven and takes only a short while to cook.

Serves 6
Preparation time: 12 minutes
Cooking time: Microwave cookery 9 minutes

### Dumplings

### Ingredients

1 1/4 cups white self-raising flour 3/4 cup white self-raising flour and 1/2 cup wholemeal self-raising flour

1/2 teaspoon baking powder

30 g (1 oz) butter 30 g (1 oz) salt-reduced mono-unsaturated margarine

1/3 cup milk 1/3 cup low-fat milk

1/3 cup golden syrup 1/4 cup golden syrup

1/2 teaspoon vanilla essence

### Method

1. Sift white flour and baking powder into a medium-sized mixing bowl. Stir in wholemeal flour.
2. Rub butter margarine into dry ingredients with the tips of the fingers until mixture resembles fine breadcrumbs. This process may be done using an electric food processor.
3. Pour milk and golden syrup into a microwave-safe jug. Microwave on high for 40 seconds and stir. Stir in vanilla.

Custard Tart (see recipe opposite page)

Golden Syrup Dumplings (see recipe opposite page)

4. Make a well in the centre of the dry ingredients. Pour in milk mixture. Stir until ingredients are well combined. When substituting wholemeal flour, it may be necessary to add a little more milk to sufficiently moisten mixture. Mixture should be a moist consistency.

5. With floured hands, roll dumpling mixture into balls approximately the size of a walnut. Set dumplings aside and prepare sauce.

## Sauce

### Ingredients

30 g (1 oz) butter 30 g (1 oz) salt-reduced mono-unsaturated margarine

$^1/_2$ cup brown sugar $^1/_3$ cup brown sugar

$^1/_2$ cup golden syrup $^1/_3$ cup golden syrup

$1^1/_2$ cups water

2 teaspoons finely grated lemon rind

$^1/_2$ teaspoon vanilla essence

### Method

1. Place all the ingredients into a large microwave-safe bowl. Stir well.

2. Microwave on high for 5 minutes, stirring occasionally to dissolve sugar.

3. Place dumplings into hot sauce.

4. Cover with vented plastic wrap.

6. Microwave on high for approximately 4 minutes or until dumplings are well risen and firm.

   Serve with whipped cream omit cream, icecream reduced-fat icecream or custard (see recipe page 69) as desired.

## Ginger Pudding

Serves 6
Preparation time: 12 minutes
Cooking time: Convection cookery 2 hours
Microwave cookery 1 minute per cup

### Ingredients

1 cup white flour $^1/_2$ cup white flour and $^1/_2$ cup wholemeal flour

1 teaspoon bicarbonate of soda

1 teaspoon ground ginger

3 tablespoons sugar 2 tablespoons sugar

3 tablespoons butter 2 tablespoons salt-reduced mono-unsaturated margarine

3 tablespoons golden syrup 2 tablespoons golden syrup

$^3/_4$ cup milk $^3/_4$ cup low-fat milk

### Method

1. **Convection cookery**
   Prepare a 2 litre (4 pt) steamer with lid by spraying with cooking spray. or
   **Microwave cookery**
   Prepare approximately 6 microwave-safe teacups by spraying with cooking spray.

2. Sift white flour, bicarbonate of soda and ginger into a medium-sized mixing bowl. Stir in sugar. Stir in wholemeal flour. Rub butter margarine into dry ingredients with the tips of the fingers until mixture resembles fine bread-crumbs. This process may be done using an electric food processor.

3. **Convection cookery**
   Place golden syrup into a small saucepan. Pour in milk. Warm over a gentle heat. or
   **Microwave cookery**
   Place golden syrup into a small microwave-safe bowl. Pour in milk. Microwave on high for 40 seconds.

4. Mix liquid into dry ingredients. When substituting wholemeal flour, it may be necessary to add a little more milk to sufficiently moisten mixture. Mixture should be a batter consistency.

5. **Convection cookery**

   Pour batter into prepared steamer. Secure lid. Place steamer into a saucepan of boiling water. Water should come halfway up the sides of the steamer. Steam for 2 hours. or

   **Microwave cookery**

   Pour batter mixture into prepared cups to $^1/_3$ fill each cup. Microwave on high for approximately 1 minute per cup. Serve with cream omit cream, icecream reduced-fat icecream or custard (see recipe page 69) as desired.

## Lemon Delicious Pudding

Serves 6
Preparation time: 10 minutes
Cooking time: Convection cookery 40 minutes
Microwave cookery 10 minutes

### Ingredients

1 tablespoon butter 1 tablespoon salt-reduced mono-unsaturated margarine

125 g (4 oz) caster sugar 90 g (3 oz) caster sugar

$^1/_2$ teaspoon vanilla essence

2 eggs, separated

2 tablespoons white flour 2 tablespoons wholemeal flour

300 ml ($^1/_2$ pt) milk 300 ml ($^1/_2$ pt) low-fat milk

Finely grated rind 1 lemon

$^1/_2$ cup lemon juice (approx. 2 lemons)

### Method

1. Preheat oven to 180°C (350°F).
2. Prepare a 2 litre (4 pt) (Pyrex®) ovenproof dish by spraying with cooking spray.
3. Cream butter margarine sugar and vanilla.
4. Add egg yolks to creamed mixture one a time, beating well after each addition.
5. Sift white flour into a medium-sized mixing bowl. Stir in wholemeal flour.
6. Add flour and milk alternately to creamed mixture, beating well after each addition.
7. Stir in lemon rind and juice.

8. Place egg whites into a clean, dry bowl and beat until stiff. Lightly fold into pudding mixture and pour into prepared dish.
9. **Convection cookery**

   Place pudding dish into a larger ovenproof dish. Pour in enough cold water to go about half way up the dish. Place into a moderate oven and bake for approximately 40 minutes or until set in the centre when tested with the point of a sharp knife. When pudding is cooked carefully remove from oven. Remove pudding dish from dish of hot water and allow to cool. or

   **Microwave cookery**

   Place pudding dish into a larger microwave-safe dish. Pour in enough cold water to go about halfway up the pudding dish. Microwave on medium-high for approximately 10 minutes or until set in the centre when tested with the point of a sharp knife. When pudding is cooked carefully remove from dish of hot water and allow to cool. Serve with cream omit cream, icecream reduced-fat icecream or custard (see recipe page 69) as desired.

## Lemon Meringue Pie

Serves 6
Preparation time: 30 minutes
Cooking time: Convection cookery 15 minutes for pastry case + 10 minutes to brown meringue

## Pastry

### Ingredients

125 g (4 oz) butter 90 g (3 oz) salt-reduced mono-unsaturated margarine

90 g (3 oz) sugar 60 g (2 oz) sugar

$^1/_2$ teaspoon vanilla essence

1 egg, lightly beaten

180 g (6 oz) white flour 100 g (3 $^1/_2$ oz) white flour and 80 g (2$^1/_2$ oz) wholemeal flour

$^1/_4$ teaspoon baking powder

30 g (1 oz) cornflour

30 g (1 oz) custard powder

## Method

1. Preheat oven to 190°C (375°F).
2. Prepare a 23cm (9 in) pie plate by spraying with cooking spray.
3. Cream butter margarine, sugar and vanilla.
4. Gradually add egg to creamed mixture, beating well after each addition.
5. Sift white flour, baking powder, cornflour and custard powder into creamed mixture. Stir in wholemeal flour. Mix to a firm dough. When substituting wholemeal flour, it may be necessary to add a little milk to sufficiently moisten mixture. Mixture should be a firm consistency.
6. Turn out onto a lightly floured board and knead lightly. Roll out to 0.5 cm ($^1/_4$ in) thickness.
7. Cut a circle of pastry, 2.5 cm (1 in) larger than pie plate. Carefully line prepared pie plate with pastry. Prick base with a fork. Moisten edge of pastry with a brush dipped in water. Roll out a 1 cm ($^1/_2$ in) strip of pastry to fit around edge of pie shell. (A double thickness of pastry is needed around the edge to prevent burning during cooking.)
8. Place into a moderately hot oven and bake for approximately 15 minutes or until pale golden brown.
9. While pastry case is cooking, prepare lemon filling.

## Lemon Filling

### Ingredients

4 tablespoons cornflour
2 tablespoons white flour
1 cup water
$^1/_3$ cup sugar $^1/_4$ cup sugar
1 cup milk 1 cup low-fat milk
Finely grated rind of 1 lemon
3 egg yolks (retain whites for meringue topping)
30 g (1 oz) butter 20 g ($^3/_4$ oz) salt-reduced mono-unsaturated margarine
$^1/_2$ cup lemon juice

## Method

1. Sift cornflour and flour into a small bowl. Blend with a little of the water. Gradually stir in remainder of water. Stir in sugar, milk and lemon rind.
2. **Convection cookery**
   Pour lemon mixture into a medium-sized saucepan. Cook over a gentle heat, stirring constantly until mixture boils and thickens. Boil for 1 minute, stirring constantly to cook the flour in the mixture. or
   **Microwave cookery**
   Pour lemon mixture into a medium-sized microwave-safe bowl. Microwave on high for 1 minute and stir. Continue to microwave on high stirring at 1 minute intervals until mixture boils and thickens.
3. Remove from heat. Stir in egg yolks, butter margarine and lemon juice and mix well.
4. Cool slightly before pouring into cooked pastry case.
5. Prepare Meringue.

## Meringue

### Ingredients

3 egg whites
6 tablespoons caster sugar 4 tablespoons caster sugar

### Method

1. Increase oven temperature to 200°C (400°F).
2. Place egg whites into a large, clean, dry bowl. Beat until whites are stiff.
3. Gradually add sugar and beat well until all the sugar is dissolved.
4. Pipe or pile meringue onto lemon filling in tart case.
5. Place into a moderately hot oven and bake for approximately 10 minutes or until meringue is set and tips are golden brown. Take care not to burn tips of meringue. Serve with cream omit cream, icecream reduced-fat ice cream or custard (see recipe page 69) as desired.

Lemon Meringue (see recipe page 73)

# Lemon Sago

Serves 4
Preparation time: 5 minutes
Cooking time: Convection cookery 5 minutes
Microwave cookery 3 minutes

## Ingredients

³/₄ cup sago
3 cups boiling water
Finely grated rind and juice 1 lemon
3 tablespoons golden syrup 2 tablespoons golden syrup
3 tablespoons sugar 2 tablespoons sugar

## Method

1. **Convection cookery**
   Place all the ingredients into a medium-sized saucepan.
   Simmer until sago is clear and mixture thickens. or
   **Microwave cookery**
   Place all the ingredients into a medium-sized microwave-safe bowl. Microwave on high for 1 minute and stir.
   Continue to microwave on medium-high, stirring at
   1-minute intervals until sago is clear and mixture thickens.
   Serve with cream omit cream, icecream reduced-fat ice-cream or custard (see recipe page 69 as desired.

# Marshmallow Pavlova

This pavlova has a delicious soft, melt-in-the-mouth centre around a lightly crisp base. If you wish to have a crisp pavlova, see recipe for pavolva on page 77.

Serves 6-8
Preparation time: 20 minutes
Cooking time: Convection cookery 1¹/₂ hours
(Pavlova needs to be left in the oven to cool.)

## Ingredients

4 egg whites
1 cup caster sugar ³/₄ cup caster sugar
¹/₂ teaspoon vanilla essence
¹/₂ teaspoon white vinegar

## Method

1. Preheat oven to 120°C (250°F).
2. Prepare a pavlova tray or flat ovenproof plate by spraying with cooking spray.
3. Place egg whites into a large, clean, dry bowl. Beat until whites are stiff.
4. Add ¹/₄ cup of sugar and beat until sugar dissolves. Gradually add remainder of sugar beating well after each addition.
5. Mix in vanilla and vinegar.
6. Pile onto prepared tray and shape as desired taking care not to spread the mixture any larger than an 18 cm (7 in) circle as the pavlova will spread during cooking. Build up the sides of the pavlova to a height of 7.5 cm (3 in). Smooth the sides and top of pavlova. Make a decorative edge around pavlova with a flat-bladed knife if desired.
7. Place into a slow oven and bake for approximately 1¹/₂ hours. Pavlova should be firm to touch on the outside. Turn oven off and leave in oven to cool. When pavlova is quite cold it is ready to use.
8. Using a sharp pointed knife, cut a circle around the top of the pavlova, allowing the crisp meringue to fall slightly into the soft centre of the pavlova. This will allow room to top with fresh strawberries and whipped cream as desired omit cream.
   Serve with cream omit cream, ice cream, reduced-fat icecream fresh fruit or custard (see recipe page 69) as desired.

## Pavlova

This pavlova case is crisp throughout. If you wish to have a soft-centred pavlova, see recipe for Marshmallow Pavlova on page 76. Choose a suitable baking tray that can be used as a serving plate, as it may be too difficult to remove Pavlova to another plate for serving.

Serves 10
Preparation time: 20 minutes
Cooking time: Convection cookery 1$^1$/$_2$ hours (Pavlova needs to be left in the oven overnight to dry out.)

### Ingredients

2 cups caster sugar 1$^1$/$_2$ cups caster sugar

2 egg whites

1 teaspoon white vinegar

2 tablespoons boiling water

2 teaspoons cornflour

$^1$/$_2$ teaspoon baking powder

$^1$/$_4$ teaspoon vanilla essence

### Method

1. Preheat oven to 200°C (400°F).
2. Prepare a 30 cm (12 in) pavlova tray or flat ovenproof plate by spraying with cooking spray.
3. Place caster sugar, egg whites, vinegar and boiling water into a large bowl. Beat until mixture is stiff enough to hold its own peaks. It is best to use a heavy-duty electric mixer for this process.
4. Sift cornflour and baking powder into bowl. Stir into egg white mixture.
5. Stir in vanilla.
6. Pile onto prepared tray and shape as desired.
7. Place into oven and immediately reduce heat to 150°C (300°F) for 30 minutes to dry out pavlova. Reduce heat to 100°C (225°F) for 1 hour longer. Turn off oven and leave pavlova in oven overnight to dry out.
   For serving, fill pavlova case with fruit salad and freshly whipped cream omit cream.
   The pavlova case will keep for up to one month if stored in an airtight container.

## Trifle

Serves 8
Preparation time: 45 minutes
As the orange cake and the custard must be cold, it is best to make them ahead of time. Trifle needs to be refrigerated for at least 1 hour before serving, to allow flavour to develop.

### Ingredients

1 layer of Orange Cake (see recipe page 90)

4 tablespoons cream sherry

1 x 440 g (15 oz) can mango pieces in natural juice or 440 g 15 oz) fresh mango pieces can be substituted as desired

1 quantity custard (see recipe page 69)

1 x 440 g (15 oz) can pineapple pieces in natural juice

1 x 440 g (15 oz) can paw paw pieces in natural juice or 440g (15 oz) fresh paw paw pieces can be substituted as desired

1 cup cream omit cream

2 kiwifruit

2 passionfruit

### Method

1. Cut orange cake into 3 cm (1 in) cubes. Arrange in the bottom of a large glass serving bowl. Pour sherry over cake.
2. Place mango pieces into a medium-sized bowl and mash to a pulp. Stir in cold custard. Pour mango custard over cake. Allow to soak completely into cake.
3. Place pineapple and paw paw over cake.
4. Refrigerate for at least 1 hour or until required.
5. Just before serving, top with whipped cream omit cream.
6. Peel and slice kiwi fruit and place on top of trifle.
7. Remove pulp from passionfruit and pour over trifle.

## Pineapple Upside-down Cake

Preparation time: 12 minutes
Cooking time: Convection cookery 30 minutes
Microwave cookery 8 minutes

### Ingredients (for base of tin)

125 g (4 oz) butter 90 g (3 oz) salt-reduced mono-unsaturated
margarine
180 g (6 oz) brown sugar 150 g (5 oz) brown sugar
1/2 teaspoon vanilla
1 x 440 g (15 oz) can pineapple rings in natural juice (strain juice
and reserve for cake mixture)
10 glace cherries omit cherries if you wish to reduce sugar intake

### Method

1. Prepare an 18 cm (7 in) round cake tin by spraying with
   cooking spray. (If cake is to be cooked in the microwave,
   use a ring-shaped microwave-safe cake container.)
2. **Convection cookery**
   Place butter margarine into a small saucepan and melt over
   a gentle heat. Remove from heat. or
   **Microwave cookery**
   Place butter margarine into a small microwave-safe bowl.
   Cover and microwave on high for 40 seconds or until butter
   margarine is melted.
3. Mix sugar and vanilla into melted butter margarine and
   pour over base of prepared tin.
4. Carefully arrange pineapple rings and cherries omit cherries
   if desired in tin, on top of brown sugar mixture.

Pineapple Upside-down Cake
(see recipe above)

# Cake mixture

## Ingredients

60 g (2 oz) butter 40 g (1½ oz) salt-reduced mono-unsaturated margarine

½ cup caster sugar ⅓ cup caster sugar

½ teaspoon vanilla essence

1 egg, lightly beaten

1½ cups white self-raising flour ¾ cup white self-raising flour and ¾ cup wholemeal self-raising flour

3 tablespoons reserved pineapple juice

## Method

1. Preheat oven to 180°C (350°F).
2. Cream butter margarine, sugar and vanilla.
3. Gradually add egg to creamed mixture, beating well after each addition.
4. Sift white flour into creamed mixture and mix well. Add pineapple juice and stir well. Stir in wholemeal flour. When substituting wholemeal flour, it may be necessary to add a little more pineapple juice to sufficiently moisten mixture. Mixture should be a moist consistency.
5. Carefully spread over pineapple in tin.
6. **Convection cookery**
   Place into a moderate oven and bake for approximately 30 minutes or until cooked when tested. or
   **Microwave cookery**
   Microwave on high for approximately 8 minutes or until cooked in the centre when tested.
7. Allow to remain in tin for 5 minutes before turning onto a serving plate to cool.
   Serve with cream omit cream, icecream reduced-fat icecream or custard (see recipe page 69).

# Treacle Pudding

Serves 6
Preparation time: 12 minutes
Cooking time: Convection cookery 2 hours
Microwave cookery 1 minute per cup

## Ingredients

2 tablespoons dripping 1 tablespoon salt-reduced mono-unsaturated margarine

3 tablespoons caster sugar 2 tablespoons caster sugar

3 tablespoons treacle 2 tablespoons treacle

½ teaspoon vanilla essence

1 cup milk 1 cup low-fat milk

2 cups white flour 1 cup white flour and 1 cup wholemeal flour

1 teaspoon bicarbonate of soda

2 teaspoons ground ginger

## Method

1. **Convection cookery**
   Prepare a 2 litre (4 pt) pudding steamer by spraying with cooking spray. or
   **Microwave cookery**
   Prepare approximately 6 microwave-safe cups by spraying with cooking spray.
2. Cream dripping margarine, sugar and treacle. Stir in vanilla.
3. **Convection cookery**
   Pour milk into a small saucepan. Warm over a gentle heat. or
   **Microwave cookery**
   Pour milk into a small microwave-safe bowl. Microwave on high for 40 seconds to warm milk.
4. Sift white flour, bicarbonate of soda and ginger into a medium-sized bowl. Stir in wholemeal flour.
5. Stir dry ingredients and milk alternately into creamed mixture mixing well after each addition. When substituting wholemeal flour, it may be necessary to add a little more milk to sufficiently moisten mixture. Mixture should be a batter consistency.

79

6. Convection cookery Pour batter into prepared steamer. Secure lid. Place steamer into a saucepan of boiling water. Water should come halfway up the sides of the steamer. Steam for 2 hours. or

   **Microwave cookery**

   Pour batter into prepared cups to $^1/_3$ fill each cup. Microwave on high for approximately 1 minute per cup. Serve with cream omit cream, icecream reduced-fat ice-cream or custard (see recipe page 69) as desired.

## Treacle Tart

Serves 6
Preparation time: 20 minutes
Cooking time: Convection cookery 35 minutes

## Treacle Filling

### Ingredients

$^1/_2$ cup treacle $^1/_3$cup treacle
2 teaspoons finely grated lemon rind
1$^1/_4$ cups breadcrumbs 1$^1/_4$ cups wholemeal breadcrumbs

### Method

1. **Convection cookery**

   Place all the ingredients into a small saucepan. Cook over a low heat, stirring continuously to combine ingredients. Remove from heat. or

   **Microwave cookery**

   Place all the ingredients into a small microwave-safe bowl. Microwave on high for 1 minute and stir. Microwave on high for a further minute and stir.

2. Set filling aside while preparing pastry.

## Pastry

### Ingredients

I cup white flour $^1/_2$ cup white flour and $^1/_2$ cup wholemeal flour
I teaspoon baking powder
$^1/_2$ cup ground rice
90 g (3 oz) butter 60 g (2 oz) salt-reduced mono-unsaturated margarine
$^1/_2$ cup caster sugar
100 ml (3$^1/_2$ fl oz) milk 100 ml (3$^1/_2$ fl oz) low-fat milk

### Method

1. Preheat oven to 180°C (350°F).
2. Prepare a 23 cm (9 in) tart plate by spraying with cooking spray.
3. Sift flour and baking powder into a medium-sized mixing bowl. Stir in wholemeal flour. Stir in ground rice. Rub butter margarine into dry ingredients with the tips of the fingers until mixture resembles fine breadcrumbs. This process may be done using an electric food processor.
4. Stir in sugar.
5. Stir in sufficient milk to mix to a firm dough. When substituting wholemeal flour, it may be necessary to add a little more milk to sufficiently moisten dough. Dough should be a firm consistency.
6. Turn dough out onto a lightly floured board and knead lightly.
7. Gently roll out dough to approximately 0.5 cm ($^1/_4$ in) thickness.
8. Carefully line base of prepared tart plate with pastry, reserving enough pastry to decorate top of tart.
9. Pour filling onto prepared tart base.
10. Cut remaining pastry into 1 cm ($^1/_2$ in) wide strips and decorate top of tart.
11. Place tart into a moderate oven and bake for approximately 35 minutes or until firm to touch and lightly golden brown. Delicious served hot or cold with cream omit cream, icecream reduced-fat icecream or custard (see recipe page 69).

# Cakes *Cakes*

## Banana Cake

Preparation time: 20 minutes
Cooking time: Convection cookery 45 minutes
Microwave cookery 10 minutes

### Ingredients
125 g (4 oz) butter 90 g (3 oz) salt-reduced mono-unsaturated margarine

180 g (6 oz) caster sugar 150 g (5 oz) caster sugar
1/2 teaspoon vanilla essence
2 eggs, lightly beaten
3 bananas, mashed (Bananas must be ripe to make a good banana cake.)
1¹/₂ cups white flour ¹/₂ cup white flour and 1 cup wholemeal flour
1 teaspoon baking powder
¹/₂ teaspoon bicarbonate of soda
1 teaspoon ground cinnamon
¹/₂ cup milk ¹/₂ cup low-fat milk

### Method
1. Preheat oven to 160°C (325°F).
2. Prepare a 23 cm x 13 cm (9 in x 5 in) loaf cake tin by spraying with cooking spray. (If cake is to be cooked in the microwave, use a ring-shaped microwave-safe cake container.)
3. Cream butter margarine, sugar and vanilla.
4. Gradually add egg to creamed mixture, beating well after each addition.
5. Beat in mashed banana a little at a time, beating well after each addition.
6. Sift white flour, baking powder, bicarbonate of soda and cinnamon into a medium-sized bowl and stir well. Stir in wholemeal flour.
7. Mix dry ingredients and milk alternately into creamed mixture, mixing well after each addition. When substituting wholemeal flour, it may be necessary to add a little more milk to sufficiently moisten mixture. Mixture should be a moist consistency.
8. Spread mixture into prepared tin.
9. **Convection cookery**
   Place into a moderate oven and bake for approximately 45 minutes or until cooked in the centre when tested. or
   **Microwave cookery**
   Microwave on high for 7 minutes. Continue to microwave on medium for 3 minutes or until cooked when tested.
10. Leave in tin for 5 minutes before turning out onto a fine wire rack to cool.
    When the cake is cold, ice with vanilla icing and sprinkle with cinnamon. Omit vanilla icing and sprinkle with cinnamon.

## Apple Teacake

Preparation time: 20 minutes
Cooking time: Convection cookery 30 – 40 minutes
Microwave cookery 7 minutes

### Ingredients
1 tablespoon butter 1 tablespoon salt-reduced mono-unsaturated margarine
¹/₂ cup sugar ¹/₃ cup sugar
¹/₂ teaspoon vanilla essence

I egg, lightly beaten

$^1/_2$ cup milk $^1/_2$ cup low-fat milk

I cup white flour $^1/_2$ cup white flour and $^1/_2$ cup wholemeal flour

I teaspoon baking powder

I large cooking apple

Ground cinnamon (to sprinkle on top)

Caster sugar (to sprinkle on top) omit caster sugar

## Method

1. Preheat oven to 180°C (350°F).
2. Prepare an 18 cm (7 in) round cake tin by spraying with cooking spray. (If cake is to be cooked in the microwave, use a ring-shaped microwave-safe cake container.)
3. Cream butter margarine, sugar and vanilla.
4. Gradually add egg to creamed mixture, beating well after each addition.
5. Stir in half the milk.
6. Sift white flour and baking powder into mixture and stir in well.
7. Stir in remainder of the milk. Stir in wholemeal flour. When substituting wholemeal flour, it may be necessary to add a little more milk to sufficiently moisten mixture. Mixture should be a moist consistency.
8. Spread mixture into prepared tin.
9. Peel and thinly slice apple. Arrange slices on top of mixture.
10. **Convection cookery**
    Place into a moderate oven and bake for approximately 35-40 minutes or until cooked in the centre when tested. or
    **Microwave cookery**
    Microwave on high for 5 minutes. Continue to microwave on medium for 2 minutes or until cooked when tested.
11. Leave in tin for 5 minutes before turning out onto a fine wire rack to cool.

# Boiled Fruitcake

Preparation time: 30 minutes

Cooking time: Convection cookery $2^1/_2$ hours

Microwave cookery 9 minutes

## Ingredients

250 g (8 oz) butter 180 g (6 oz) salt-reduced mono-unsaturated margarine

2 cups raw sugar $1^1/_2$ cups raw sugar

2 cups water

I tablespoon treacle

$^1/_2$ teaspoon vanilla essence

250 g (8 oz) sultanas natural sultanas

250 g (8 oz) raisins natural raisins, finely chopped

125 g (4 oz) dried apricots (finely chopped)

60 g (2 oz) currants

60 g (2 oz) walnut pieces, finely chopped

3 eggs, lightly beaten

I cup wheat germ

2 cups white flour 2 cups wholemeal flour

I cup white self-raising flour I cup wholemeal self-raising flour

$^1/_2$ teaspoon ground cinnamon

$^1/_4$ teaspoon ground nutmeg

2 tablespoons brandy

## Method

1. Preheat oven to 160°C (325°F).
2. Prepare a 23 cm (9 in) square cake tin by spraying with cooking spray. Line base and sides of tin with baking paper. (If cake is to be cooked in the microwave, use a ring-shaped microwave-safe cake container.)
3. **Convection cookery**
   Place butter margarine, sugar, water, treacle, vanilla, sultanas, raisins, apricots, currants and walnuts into a large saucepan. Stir over a low heat. Bring to the boil. Reduce heat and boil gently, with lid off, for 3 minutes. or
   **Microwave cookery**
   Place butter margarine, sugar, water, treacle, vanilla, sultanas, raisins, apricots, currants and walnuts into a large microwave-safe bowl. Microwave on high for 2 minutes and

Apple Teacake (see recipe page 81)

Christmas Pudding with Brandy Sauce (see recipe page 68)

stir. Microwave for a further 2 minutes.

4. Allow mixture to cool. It is important that the mixture be cool before proceeding.

5. Stir in egg. Stir in wheat germ. Sift white flour stir wholemeal flour, cinnamon and nutmeg into mixture. Mix well. When substituting wholemeal flour, it may be necessary to add a little milk to sufficiently moisten mixture. Mixture should be a moist consistency.

6. Spread mixture into prepared tin.

7. **Convection cookery**
Place into a moderately slow oven and bake for approximately 2$^1$/$_2$ hours or until cooked in the centre when tested. It may be necessary to cover cake with a sheet of brown paper during baking to prevent the surface burning. or
**Microwave cookery**
Microwave on high for 5 minutes. Continue to microwave on medium for 4 minutes or until cooked when tested.

8. When cooked, carefully pour brandy over cake.

9. When cold, remove cake from tin and wrap in foil. Cake is best stored in the refrigerator. Boiled fruitcake will not keep as well as traditional fruitcake.

## Butter Cake

Preparation time: 12 minutes
Cooking time: Convection cookery 35 minutes
Microwave cookery 8 minutes

### Ingredients
125 g (4 oz) butter 90 g (3 oz) salt-reduced mono-unsaturated margarine
$^3$/$_4$ cup caster sugar $^1$/$_2$ cup caster sugar
$^1$/$_2$ teaspoon vanilla essence
2 eggs, lightly beaten
1$^1$/$_2$ cups white flour $^1$/$_2$ cup white flour and 1 cup wholemeal flour
1$^1$/$_2$ teaspoons baking powder
$^3$/$_4$ cup milk $^3$/$_4$ cup low-fat milk

**Method**

1. Preheat oven to 180°C (350°F).

2. Prepare an 18 cm (7 in) round cake tin by spraying with cooking spray. (If cake is to be cooked in the microwave, use a ring-shaped microwave-safe cake container.)

3. Cream butter margarine, sugar and vanilla.

4. Gradually add egg to creamed mixture, beating well after each addition.

5. Sift white flour and baking powder into a medium-sized bowl and mix well. Stir in wholemeal flour.

6. Stir dry ingredients and milk alternately into creamed mixture, mixing well after each addition. When substituting wholemeal flour, it may be necessary to add a little more milk to sufficiently moisten mixture. Mixture should be a moist consistency.

7. Spread mixture into prepared tin.

8. **Convection cookery**
Place into a moderate oven and bake for approximately 30-35 minutes or until cooked in the centre when tested. or
**Microwave cookery**
Microwave on high for 5 minutes. Continue to microwave on medium for 3 minutes or until cooked when tested.

9. Leave in tin for 5 minutes before turning out onto a fine wire rack to cool.

## Carrot Cake

Preparation time: 20 minutes
Cooking time: Convection cookery 45 minutes
Microwave cookery 9 minutes

### Ingredients
1$^3$/$_4$ cups sugar 1$^1$/$_2$ cups sugar
4 eggs 3 eggs, lightly beaten
2 teaspoons ground cinnamon
$^1$/$_2$ teaspoon vanilla essence
1$^1$/$_2$ cups salad oil 1 cup canola or olive oil
3 carrots, finely grated
1 cup walnut pieces, finely chopped
1 cup sultanas natural sultanas
2 cups white flour 1 cup white flour and 1 cup wholemeal flour
2 teaspoons bicarbonate of soda

**Method**

1. Preheat oven to 180°C (350°F).
2. Prepare a 23 cm (9 in) round cake tin by spraying with cooking spray. Line base of tin with baking paper. (If cake is to be cooked in the microwave, use a ring-shaped microwave-safe cake container.)
3. Combine sugar, eggs, cinnamon, vanilla, oil and carrot in a mixing bowl. Beat at a slow speed for 2 minutes.
4. Fold in walnuts and sultanas.
5. Sift white flour and bicarbonate of soda into mixture and stir in well. Stir in wholemeal flour. When substituting wholemeal flour, it may be necessary to add a little milk to sufficiently moisten mixture. Mixture should be a very moist consistency.
6. Spread mixture into prepared tin.
7. **Convection cookery**
   Place into a moderate oven and bake for approximately 45 minutes or until cooked in the centre when tested. or
   **Microwave cookery**
   Microwave on high for 6 minutes. Continue to microwave on medium for 3 minutes or until cooked when tested.
8. Leave in tin for 5 minutes before turning out onto a fine wire rack to cool.

Carrot Cake
(see recipe opposite page)

85

## Chocolate-Banana Cake (Gluten-free)

This recipe is designed for those who need to follow a gluten-free diet. This is a very easy cake to make as it is mixed in a food processor. It is a delicious moist cake. It is best stored in the refrigerator.

Preparation time: 10 minutes
Cooking time: Convection cookery 45 minutes
Microwave cookery 8 minutes

### Ingredients

1 ripe banana
1/2 cup brown rice flour
1/4 cup white rice flour
1/4 cup cornflour (gluten-free)
1/4 cup custard powder (gluten-free)
1/2 cup gluten-free plain flour
1/2 cup cocoa
1 teaspoon bicarbonate of soda
1 1/4 cups brown sugar
2/3 cup canola oil 1/2 cup canola or olive oil
1 tablespoon white vinegar
1 cup buttermilk
2 eggs
2 tablespoons strawberry jam
1 teaspoon vanilla essence

### Method

1. Preheat oven to 180°C (350°F).
2. Prepare a 23 cm (9 in) round fluted ring cake tin by spraying with cooking spray. (If cake is to be cooked in the microwave, use a ring-shaped microwave-safe cake container.)
3. Peel banana and place into food processor.
4. Add remaining ingredients and blend until well combined.
5. Spread mixture into prepared tin.
6. **Convection cookery**
   Place into a moderate oven and bake for 15 minutes. Reduce heat to 150°C (300°F) for a further 30 minutes or until cooked when tested. or

Microwave cookery
Microwave on high for 5 minutes. Continue to microwave on medium-high for 3 minutes or until cooked when tested.

7. Remove from oven and leave in tin for 10 minutes before turning out onto a fine wire rack to cool.

## Christmas Cake

Preparation time: 30 minutes
Cooking time: Convection cookery 3 hours
Microwave cookery 15 minutes
The brandy can be poured over the fruit and stored in a sealed container for several weeks. The longer it is left the better the development of the flavour.

### Ingredients

250 g (8 oz) raisins natural raisins, finely chopped
250 g (8 oz) sultanas natural sultanas
250 g (8 oz) currants
125 g (4 oz) mixed peel
125 g (4 oz) blanched almonds, chopped
Finely grated rind of 1 orange
Finely grated rind of 1 lemon
2 tablespoons marmalade (see recipe page 14)
2/3 cup brandy
250 g (8 oz) butter 180 g (6 oz) salt-reduced mono-unsaturated margarine
250 g (8 oz) brown sugar 200 g (7 oz) brown sugar
1 teaspoon vanilla essence
4 eggs, use 3 whole eggs and 1 egg white, lightly beaten
2 tablespoons treacle
350 g (11 oz) white flour 350 g (11 oz) wholemeal flour
60 g (2 oz) white self-raising flour 60 (2 oz) wholemeal self-raising flour
1/2 teaspoon ground nutmeg
1/2 teaspoon ground cinnamon
1 teaspoon mixed spice
2 tablespoons brandy (extra, to pour over cake when it is cooked)

## Method

1. Preheat oven to 150°C (300°F).
2. Prepare a 23 cm (9 in) round cake tin by spraying with cooking spray. Line inside base and sides of tin with baking paper. Wrap 3 thicknesses of brown paper around base and sides of tin. This is done to promote even cooking. (If cake is to be cooked in the microwave, use a large ring-shaped microwave-safe cake container.)
3. Mix together all the fruits, peel, almonds, rinds and marmalade in a large bowl. Pour in brandy. (For best results seal and leave for several weeks.)
4. Cream butter margarine, sugar and vanilla.
5. Gradually add egg to creamed mixture, beating well after each addition.
6. Stir in treacle.
7. Sift white flour, nutmeg, cinnamon and spice into a medium-sized bowl and mix well. Stir in wholemeal flour.
8. Add half the dry ingredients and stir well.
9. Add half the fruit mixture and stir well.
10. Add remainder of dry ingredients and stir well.
11. Add remainder of the fruit mixture and mix thoroughly. When substituting wholemeal flour, it may be necessary to add a little milk to sufficiently moisten mixture. Mixture should be a moist consistency.
12. Spread mixture into prepared tin. Smooth surface with a moistened spatula.
13. **Convection cookery**
    Place into a slow oven and bake for 30 minutes. Reduce heat to 120°C (250°F) and bake for a further 2 hours. Remove brown paper from top of cake and bake for a further 30 minutes or until cooked in the centre when tested. or
    **Microwave cookery**
    Microwave on high for 5 minutes. Continue to microwave on medium for 10 minutes or until cooked when tested.
14. When cooked, remove from oven. Slowly pour extra 2 tablespoons of brandy over top of cake in tin.
15. Place a sheet of greaseproof or brown paper on top of cake in tin and wrap in several thicknesses of newspaper.
16. Allow to cool overnight before unwrapping.

# Date Loaf

Preparation time: 8 minutes + about 15 minutes for boiling water to cool after it has been poured over dates. This can be done ahead of time.
Cooking time: Convection cookery 45 minutes
Microwave cookery 8 minutes

## Ingredients

1 cup finely chopped dates
$^1/_2$ teaspoon bicarbonate of soda
1 cup boiling water
1 tablespoon butter 1 tablespoon salt-reduced mono-unsaturated margarine
$^3/_4$ cup brown sugar $^1/_2$ cup brown sugar
$^1/_2$ teaspoon vanilla essence
1 egg, lightly beaten
$1^1/_2$ cups white self-raising flour $^1/_2$ cup white self-raising flour and 1 cup wholemeal self-raising flour

## Method

1. Preheat oven to 170°C (340°F).
2. Prepare a 23 cm x 13 cm (9 in x 5 in) loaf tin by spraying with cooking spray. (If cake is to be cooked in the microwave, use a ring-shaped microwave-safe container.)
3. Place dates into a medium-sized bowl. Sprinkle with bicarbe of soda. Pour boiling water over dates and cool.
4. Cream butter margarine, sugar and vanilla.
5. Gradually add egg to creamed mixture, beating well.
6. Sift white flour into creamed mixture and stir well. Stir in wholemeal flour. When substituting wholemeal flour, it may be necessary to add a little more water to sufficiently moisten mixture. Mixture should be a moist consistency.
7. Spread mixture into prepared tin.
8. **Convection cookery**
    Place into a moderate oven and bake for approximately 45 minutes or until cooked in the centre when tested. or
    **Microwave cookery**
    Microwave on high for 5 minutes. Continue to microwave on medium for 3 minutes or until cooked when tested.
9. Leave in tin for 5 minutes before turning out onto a fine wire rack to cool.

# Gingerbread

Preparation time: 12 minutes
Cooking time: Convection cookery 40 minutes
Microwave cookery 8 minutes

## Ingredients

2 tablespoons butter I tablespoon salt-reduced mono-unsaturated margarine
I cup brown sugar ³/₃ cup brown sugar
¹/₂ teaspoon vanilla essence
I egg, lightly beaten
I cup milk I cup low-fat milk
2 tablespoons treacle
2 tablespoons boiling water
I teaspoon bicarbonate of soda
2 cups white flour I cup white flour and I cup wholemeal flour
2 teaspoons ground ginger

## Method

1. Preheat oven to 180°C (350°F).
2. Prepare a 30 cm x 20 cm (12 in x 8 in) gingerbread tin by spraying with cooking spray. (If cake is to be cooked in the microwave, use a ring-shaped microwave-safe cake container.)
3. Cream butter margarine, sugar and vanilla.
4. Gradually add egg to creamed mixture, beating well after each addition.
5. **Convection cookery**
   Pour milk into a small saucepan. Warm over a gentle heat. DO NOT BOIL. or
   **Microwave cookery**
   Pour milk into a small microwave-safe bowl. Microwave on high for 40 seconds to warm milk. DO NOT BOIL.
6. Stir treacle into warm milk.
7. Pour boiling water into a cup. Add bicarbonate of soda and stir until dissolved. Add to milk and golden syrup.
8. Sift half the white flour and ginger into creamed mixture and stir well.
9. Stir in half the liquid.
10. Sift in remainder of white flour and ginger and mix well.

11. Stir in remainder of liquid. Stir in wholemeal flour. When substituting wholemeal flour, it may be necessary to add a little more milk to sufficiently moisten mixture. Mixture should be a batter consistency.
12. Pour mixture into prepared tin.
13. **Convection cookery**
    Place into a moderate oven and bake for approximately 40 minutes or until cooked in the centre when tested. or
    **Microwave cookery**
    Microwave on high for 5 minutes. Continue to microwave on medium for 3 minutes or until cooked when tested.
14. Leave in tin for 5 minutes before turning out onto a fine wire rack to cool.

# Jam Roll

Preparation time: 12 minutes
Cooking time: Convection cookery 12 minutes

## Ingredients

3 eggs, lightly beaten
125 g (4 oz) caster sugar 100 g (3¹/₂ oz) caster sugar
90 g (3 oz) white flour 60 g (2 oz) white flour and 30 g (I oz) wholemeal flour
30 g (I oz) cornflour
I teaspoon baking powder
I teaspoon butter I teaspoon salt-reduced mono-unsaturated margarine
4 tablespoons milk 4 tablespoons low-fat milk
¹/₂ teaspoon vanilla essence
Caster sugar (extra for rolling)
Jam of your choice to put in roll use jam with no added sugar as desired (If jam is stiff, it may need to be softened for a few seconds in the microwave.)

## Method

1. Preheat oven to 190°C (375°F).
2. Prepare a 30 cm x 26 cm (12 in x 10¹/₂ in) jam roll cake tin by spraying with cooking spray. Line tin with baking paper.
3. Place eggs into the large bowl of an electric mixer. Add castor sugar and beat well for 10 minutes.

4. Sift white flour, cornflour and baking powder into mixture. Lightly fold into mixture. Stir in wholemeal flour. When substituting wholemeal flour, it may be necessary to add a little more milk to sufficiently moisten mixture. Mixture should be a moist consistency.

5. **Convection cookery**

   Place butter margarine into a small saucepan. Melt over a gentle heat. Add milk and warm gently. Stir in vanilla. or

   **Microwave cookery**

   Place butter margarine into a small microwave-safe bowl. Cover and microwave on high for 40 seconds or until butter margarine is melted. Add milk and microwave for a further 40 seconds. Stir in vanilla.

6. Lightly stir warm liquid into egg mixture.

7. Spread mixture into prepared tin.

8. Place into a moderate oven and bake for 12 minutes or until cooked when tested.

9. Have ready, a slightly dampened tea towel laid out on a flat surface. Place a sheet of baking paper over the tea towel. Sprinkle paper with caster sugar.

10. When cooked, run a sharp knife around the cake in the tin. Remove cake from tin and turn out onto caster sugar on paper. Remove baking paper from base of cake.

11. Trim 0.5 cm ($^1/_4$ in) off the edges of the cake with a sharp knife. (This only needs to be done if the edges are too crisp when cooked to form a roll.)

12. Roll up firmly and leave for 10 minutes.

13. Unroll and spread with jam.

14. Roll up and serve as desired.

## Mud Cake

This is a very dense, moist cake. It is best stored in the refrigerator.

Preparation time: 20 minutes
Cooking time: Convection cookery 75 minutes

### Ingredients

250 g (8 oz) butter 180 g (6 oz) salt-reduced mono-unsaturated margarine

150 g (5 oz) dark cooking chocolate 100 g (3$^1/_2$ oz) dark cooking chocolate

2 cups caster sugar 1$^1/_2$ cups caster sugar

1 cup hot water

1 tablespoon instant coffee powder

$^1/_3$ cup whisky

1$^3/_4$ cups white flour 1 cup white flour and $^3/_4$ cup wholemeal flour

3 tablespoons white self-raising flour

$^1/_4$ cup cocoa

2 eggs 1 whole egg and 1 egg white, lightly beaten

### Method

1. Preheat oven to 150°C (300°F).

2. Prepare a 23 cm (9 in) square slab tin by lining with baking paper.

3. **Convection cookery**

   Combine butter margarine, chocolate, sugar, water and coffee in a medium-sized saucepan. Stir over a gentle heat until chocolate is melted. Do not have the temperature too high or the chocolate will be ruined. Stir well. or

   **Microwave cookery**

   Combine butter margarine, chocolate, sugar, water and coffee in a medium-sized microwave-safe bowl. Microwave on high for 1 minute and stir. Continue to microwave on high for 20-second intervals until chocolate is melted. Stir well.

4. Allow mixture to cool.

5. Stir in whisky.

6. Sift white flour and cocoa into liquid and mix well. Stir in wholemeal flour.

7. Add lightly beaten egg and beat mixture well using an electric food mixer. When substituting wholemeal flour, it may be necessary to add a little more water to mixture. Mixture should be a runny consistency.

8. Pour mixture into prepared tin.

9. Place into a moderately slow oven and bake for approximately 1$^1/_4$ hours or until cooked in the centre when tested.

10. Leave in tin to cool.

## Orange Cake

Preparation time: 20 minutes
Cooking time: Convection cookery 40 minutes
Microwave cookery 8 minutes

### Ingredients

125 g (4 oz) butter 90 g (3 oz) salt-reduced mono-unsaturated margarine
125 g (4 oz) caster sugar 100 g (3¹/₂ oz) caster sugar
¹/₂ teaspoon vanilla essence
2 eggs, lightly beaten
1 orange
170 g (5¹/₂ oz) white flour 100 g (3 ¹/₂ oz) white flour and 70 g (2 oz) wholemeal flour
1 teaspoon baking powder
2 tablespoons milk 2 tablespoons low-fat milk

### Method

1. Preheat oven to 180°C (350°F).
2. Prepare an 18 cm (7 in) round cake tin by spraying with cooking spray. (If cake is to be cooked in the microwave, use a ring-shaped microwave-safe cake container.)
3. Cream butter margarine, sugar and vanilla.
4. Gradually add egg to creamed mixture, beating well after each addition.
5. Finely grate rind of orange. Stir into creamed mixture.
6. Squeeze juice of half the orange and stir into creamed mixture.
7. Sift half the white flour and baking powder into creamed mixture and stir well.
8. Stir in half the milk.
9. Sift in remainder of white flour and baking powder and stir well.
10. Stir in remainder of the milk. Stir in wholemeal flour. When substituting wholemeal flour, it may be necessary to add a little more milk to sufficiently moisten mixture. Mixture should be a moist consistency.
11. Spread into prepared tin.
12. **Convection cookery**
    Place into a moderate oven and bake for approximately 40 minutes or until cooked in the centre when tested. or
    **Microwave cookery**
    Microwave on high for 5 minutes. Continue to microwave on medium for 3 minutes or until cooked when tested.
13. Leave in tin for 5 minutes before turning out onto a fine wire rack to cool.


Note: The juice of the other half of the orange can be used to make orange icing. Instead of making icing, cut small pieces of orange from the other half of the orange to decorate the top of the cake.

## Yoghurt Chocolate Cake

Preparation time: 12 minutes
Cooking time: Convection cookery 40 minutes
Microwave cookery 8 minutes

### Ingredients

¹/₂ cup butter ¹/₃ cup salt-reduced mono-unsaturated margarine
1¹/₂ cups caster sugar 1 cup caster sugar
¹/₂ teaspoon vanilla essence
3 eggs 2 whole eggs and 1 egg white, lightly beaten
1 cup plain yoghurt 1 cup plain low-fat yoghurt
¹/₂ teaspoon bicarbonate of soda
2 cups white self-raising flour 1 cup white self-raising flour and 1 cup wholemeal self-raising flour
2 tablespoons cocoa
¹/₂ cup hot water

### Method

1. Preheat oven to 180°C (350°F).
2. Prepare two 18 cm (7 in) round cake tins by spraying with cooking spray. Line bottom of tins with baking paper. (If cake is to be cooked in the microwave, use a large ring-shaped microwave-safe cake container.)
3. Cream butter margarine, sugar and vanilla.
4. Gradually add egg to creamed mixture, beating well after each addition.
5. Pour yoghurt into a small bowl. Stir in bicarbonate of soda. Stir half into cake mixture.

Orange Cake
(see recipe opposite page)

7. Sift white flour into mixture and stir in well. Stir in wholemeal flour.

8. Stir in remainder of yoghurt.

9. Place cocoa into a small bowl. Mix to a smooth paste with hot water. Stir into creamed mixture. When substituting wholemeal flour, it may be necessary to add a little milk to sufficiently moisten mixture. Mixture should be a moist consistency.

10. Spread mixture into prepared tins.

11. **Convection cookery**
    Place into a moderate oven and bake for approximately 40 minutes or until cooked in the centre when tested. or
    **Microwave cookery**
    Microwave on high for 5 minutes. Continue to microwave on medium for 3 minutes or until cooked when tested.

12. Leave in tins for 10 minutes before turning out onto a fine wire rack to cool.

# Hot*Bake*

## Almond Bread

This is a crispbread that is traditionally served at Christmas. It will remain crisp when stored in an airtight container.

Makes approximately 24 slices
Preparation time: 10 minutes
Cooking time: Convection cookery 40 minutes (plus $1^1/_2$ hours for drying)

### Ingredients
3 egg whites
$^1/_2$ cup caster sugar $^1/_3$ cup caster sugar
1 cup white flour, sifted $^1/_2$ cup white flour and $^1/_4$ cup wholemeal flour
375 g (13 $^1/_2$ oz) whole almonds (with skins on)
$^1/_4$ teaspoon vanilla essence

### Method
1. Preheat oven to 150°C (300°F).
2. Prepare a 25 cm x 8 cm (10 in x 3$^1/_2$ in) bar shaped tin by spraying with cooking spray. Line tin with baking paper.
3. Place egg whites into a large clean, dry bowl. Beat until egg whites hold stiff peaks.
4. Gradually beat in caster sugar, beating well after each addition until all the sugar is thoroughly dissolved.
5. Gently fold in flour.
6. Gently stir in almonds and vanilla.
7. Spread into prepared tin.
8. Place into a moderately slow oven and bake for approximately 40 minutes or until firm to touch.
9. Allow to cool in tin for 10 minutes. Turn out onto a fine wire rack. Remove baking paper.
10. While still warm, wrap in plastic wrap.
11. Allow to cool overnight.
12. Next day, cut into 0.5 cm ($^1/_4$ in) slices.
13. Prepare 2 large flat oven trays by spraying with cooking spray. Place slices onto trays, taking care not to overlap slices.
14. Place into a very slow oven 100°C (225°F) for approximately $1^1/_2$ hours. Turn slices over approximately every 15 minutes. Cook until slices are thoroughly crisp throughout.
15. Remove from oven and allow to cool. When cold, remove from trays and store in an airtight container.

## Blueberry Muffins

Makes approximately 18 muffins
Preparation time: 7 minutes
Cooking time: Convection cookery 15 minutes

### Ingredients
250 g (8 oz) butter 180 g (6 oz) salt-reduced mono-unsaturated margarine
250 g (8 oz) caster sugar 200 g (7 oz) caster sugar
$^1/_2$ teaspoon vanilla essence
2 eggs, lightly beaten
150 g (5 oz) fresh blueberries
2$^1/_2$ cups white self-raising flour 1$^1/_2$ cups white self-raising flour and 1 cup wholemeal self-raising flour
1 cup milk 1 cup low-fat milk

Almond Bread (see recipe opposite page)

Blueberry Muffins (see recipe opposite page)

## Method

1. Preheat oven to 200°C (400°F).
2. Prepare 2 muffin tins by spraying with cooking spray.
3. Cream butter margarine, sugar and vanilla.
4. Gradually add egg to creamed mixture, beating well after each addition.
5. Wash and drain blueberries. Gently stir blueberries into mixture.
6. Sift white flour into a medium-sized mixing bowl. Stir in wholemeal flour.
7. Stir flour and milk alternately into creamed mixture, mixing well after each addition. When substituting wholemeal flour, it may be necessary to add a little more milk to sufficiently moisten mixture. Mixture should be a moist consistency.
8. Place tablespoons of mixture into prepared muffin tins.
9. Place into a moderately hot oven and bake for approximately 15 minutes or until cooked in the centre when tested.
10. When cooked, remove from oven and leave in tins for 5 minutes before turning out onto a fine wire rack to cool.


## Anzac Biscuits

One could not have a book with traditional recipes without including Anzac biscuits. The name originated during World War I when the women at home decided to send some cooking to the Anzacs, the men of the Australia and New Zealand Army Corps. This combination of ingredients was chosen because the biscuits have excellent keeping qualities. Oats is very nutritious, containing the most protein of any cereal.

Makes approximately 24 biscuits
Preparation time: 15 minutes
Cooking time: Convection cookery 15 minutes

### Ingredients

1 cup rolled oats
1 cup white flour ½ cup white flour and ½ cup wholemeal flour
1 tablespoon rice bran to increase fibre in the diet
½ cup sugar ⅓ cup raw sugar
¾ cup coconut ½ cup buckwheat kernels
125 g (4 oz) butter 90 g (3 oz) salt-reduced mono-unsaturated margarine
2 tablespoons golden syrup 1 tablespoon golden syrup
½ teaspoon bicarbonate of soda
1 tablespoon boiling water

### Method

1. Preheat oven to 160°C (325°F).
2. Prepare 2 flat oven trays by spraying with cooking spray.
3. Place rolled oats into a large mixing bowl. Sift white flour into bowl. Stir in wholemeal flour and rice bran. Stir in sugar and coconut buckwheat kernels.
4. **Convection cookery**
   Place butter margarine into a small saucepan and melt over a gentle heat. Stir in golden syrup. or
   **Microwave cookery**
   Place butter margarine into a small microwave-safe bowl. Cover and microwave on high for 40 seconds or until butter margarine is melted. Stir in golden syrup.
5. Mix bicarbonate of soda with boiling water and add to warmed liquid. Stir liquid into dry ingredients and mix well. When substituting wholemeal flour, it may be necessary to add a little more boiling water to sufficiently moisten mixture. Mixture should be a firm consistency.
6. Using lightly floured hands, roll portions of mixture into balls approximately the size of a walnut and place onto prepared trays. Use a fork dipped in flour to press flat.
7. Place into a moderately slow oven and bake for approximately 15 minutes or until golden brown.
8. When cooked, remove from oven and leave on trays for 2 minutes. Loosen biscuits and leave on trays to cool.
9. When completely cold, store in an airtight container.

Front: Brownie Squares (see recipe page 96)
Centre back: Melting Moments (see recipe page 104)
Back left and right: Anzac Biscuits (see recipe opposite page)

6. Make a well in the centre of the dry ingredients. Pour in liquid. Use a knife to stir liquid into dry ingredients. Stir from the centre to the outside and mix well. When substituting wholemeal flour, it may be necessary to add a little more milk to sufficiently moisten mixture. Mixture should be a firm consistency.
7. Turn out onto a lightly floured board and knead lightly. Pat out to 2.5 cm (1 in) thickness.
8. Dip a 3 cm (1¼ in) cutter in flour. Cut out rounds and place onto prepared tray.
9. Glaze with a little extra milk.
10. Place into a hot oven and bake for approximately 12 minutes or until golden brown and cooked.
11. When cooked, remove from oven and leave on tray for 2 minutes. Place onto a fine wire rack to cool.

## Cornflake Biscuits

Makes approximately 40 biscuits
Preparation time: 15 minutes
Cooking time: Convection cookery 12 minutes

### Ingredients
250 g (8 oz) butter 180 g (6 oz) salt-reduced mono-unsaturated margarine
1 cup caster sugar ¾ cup caster sugar
½ teaspoon vanilla essence
2 eggs, lightly beaten
2 tablespoons coconut omit coconut
½ cup chopped peanuts ¼ cup chopped peanuts
½ cup sultanas natural sultanas
2¼ cups white self-raising flour 1¼ cups white self-raising flour and 1 cup wholemeal self-raising flour
Cornflakes, crushed (for rolling)

### Method
1. Preheat oven to 180°C (350°F).
2. Prepare two biscuit trays by spraying with cooking spray.
3. Cream butter margarine, sugar and vanilla.
4. Gradually add egg to creamed mixture, beating well after each addition.

5. Stir in coconut omit coconut peanuts and sultanas.
6. Sift white flour into creamed mixture and mix well. Stir in wholemeal flour. When substituting wholemeal flour, it may be necessary to add a little milk to sufficiently moisten mixture. Mixture should be a firm consistency.
7. Roll teaspoons of mixture in crushed cornflakes.
8. Place onto prepared trays.
9. Place into a moderate oven and bake for approximately 12 minutes or until golden brown and cooked.
10. When cooked, remove from oven and leave on trays for 2 minutes. Loosen biscuits and leave on trays to cool.
11. When completely cold, store in an airtight container.

## Fruit Mince Pies

Makes approximately 24 pies
Preparation time: 30 minutes
Cooking time: Convection cookery 10 minutes
Fruit mince can be made ahead of time and stored in an airtight container in the refrigerator until required.

## Fruit Mince

### Ingredients
1 cooking apple, peeled and grated
1 x 440 g (15 oz) can crushed pineapple in natural juice
1 cup sultanas natural sultanas
1 cup chopped raisins natural raisins
½ cup currants
60 g (2 oz) glace cherries, cut in half
1 tablespoon brown sugar
1 tablespoon butter 1 teaspoon salt-reduced mono-unsaturated margarine
Finely grated rind 1 lemon
1 teaspoon ground cinnamon
½ teaspoon ground nutmeg
1 tablespoon cornflour
¼ cup brandy

Cornflake Biscuits and Orange Biscuits (see recipe page 105)

Fruit Mince Pies (see recipe opposite page)

**Method**

1. **Convection cookery**

   Place all the ingredients, except the cornflour and brandy, into a medium sized saucepan. Stir over a gentle heat until all the ingredients are well combined and mixture boils. Cook for 5 minutes over a gentle heat, stirring occasionally to prevent mixture sticking. or

   **Microwave cookery**

   Place all the ingredients except the cornflour and brandy into a medium sized microwave-safe bowl. Microwave on high for 2 minutes and stir. Microwave on medium-high stirring at 1-minute intervals until mixture is softened and well combined.

2. Place cornflour into a small bowl. Blend with brandy. Mix into hot fruit stirring continuously.

3. **Convection cookery**

   Return to heat and cook until mixture comes to the boil, stirring continuously. or

   **Microwave cookery**

   Microwave on high for 1 minute and stir. Microwave on medium for 1 minute.

4. Allow to cool and store in a covered container in the refrigerator until required as filling for Fruit Mince Pies.

## Pastry

### Ingredients

125 g (4 oz) butter 90 g (3 oz) salt-reduced mono-unsaturated margarine

$^1$/$_2$ cup caster sugar $^1$/$_3$ cup caster sugar

$^1$/$_2$ teaspoon vanilla essence

1 egg, lightly beaten

180 g (6 oz) white flour 90 g (3 oz) white flour and 90 g (3 oz) wholemeal flour

$^1$/$_2$ teaspoon baking powder

30 g (1 oz) cornflour

30 g (1 oz) custard powder

Icing sugar (to sprinkle on top of cooked pies)

**Method**

1. Preheat oven to 200°C (400°F).
2. Individual 6 cm (2$^1$/$_2$ in) foil trays are best for making these pies.
3. Cream butter margarine, sugar and vanilla.
4. Gradually add egg to creamed mixture, beating well after each addition.
5. Sift white flour, baking powder, cornflour and custard powder into creamed mixture and mix well. Stir in wholemeal flour. When substituting wholemeal flour, it may be necessary to add a little milk to sufficiently moisten dough. Dough should be a firm consistency.
6. Turn dough out onto a lightly floured board and knead lightly. Divide dough in half. Roll half the dough to approximately 0.5 cm ($^1$/$_4$ in) thickness.
7. Using a 6.5 cm (2$^3$/$_4$ in) fluted cutter dipped in flour, cut out rounds of pastry.
8. Carefully lift into individual foil trays.
9. Gently press pastry into each foil tray.
10. Place pie shells onto a flat oven tray.
11. Place 1 tablespoon fruit mince into each pie shell.
12. Roll out some pastry to approximately 0.5 cm ($^1$/$_4$ in) thickness. Using a 3 cm (1$^1$/$_4$ in) fluted cutter, cut out small rounds of pastry. Place a top onto each pie.
13. Place into a moderately hot oven and bake for 5 minutes. Reduce heat to 180°C (350°F) and bake for a further 5 minutes or until pastry is lightly golden brown.
14. When cooked, remove from oven and leave on tray to cool. Store in a covered container in the refrigerator.
15. Just before serving, lightly dust with icing sugar.

## Flapjacks

Makes approximately 30 flapjacks, depending on the individual size

Preparation time: 10 minutes
Cooking time: Convection cookery 20 minutes

### Ingredients

90 g (3 oz) butter 60 g (2 oz) salt-reduced mono-unsaturated margarine

**3 cups white self-raising flour** 1½ cups white self-raising flour and 1½ cups wholemeal self-raising flour

**¾ cup caster sugar** ½ cup caster sugar

**1¾ cups milk** 1¾ cups low-fat milk

**2 eggs,** 1 whole egg and 1 egg white **well beaten**

**½ teaspoon vanilla essence**

## Method

1. **Convection cookery**

   Place butter margarine into a small saucepan and melt over a gentle heat. or

   **Microwave cookery**

   Place butter margarine into a small microwave-safe bowl. Cover and microwave on high for 40 seconds or until butter margarine is melted.

2. Sift white flour into a large mixing bowl. Stir in sugar. Stir in wholemeal flour.

3. Pour milk into a jug. Stir in melted butter margarine, egg and vanilla.

4. Make a well in the centre of the dry ingredients. Pour in liquid and beat well, making sure there are no lumps in the mixture. When substituting wholemeal flour, it may be necessary to add a little more milk to sufficiently moisten mixture. Mixture should be a batter consistency.

5. Heat an electric frypan to 170°C (340°F). (Point no. 7 on a dial of 1-10.)

6. Spray pan with cooking spray.

7. Place tablespoons of mixture into pan.

8. Cook until bubbles appear on the surface. Turn and cook on reserve side until golden brown.

9. Place a tea towel over a fine wire rack. When cooked, remove flapjacks from frypan and place onto tea towel. Cover to prevent drying out.

   To serve, sprinkle with lemon juice and sugar use a moderate amount of sugar.

## Gingerbreads

Makes approximately 20 gingerbreads
Preparation time: 20 minutes
Cooking time: Convection cookery 15 minutes

### Ingredients

**250 g (8 oz) butter** 180 g (6 oz) salt-reduced mono-unsaturated margarine

**1 cup caster sugar** ¾ cup caster sugar

**½ teaspoon vanilla essence**

**1 whole egg and 1 egg yolk, lightly beaten**

**⅓ cup golden syrup** ¼ cup golden syrup

**4 cups white flour** 3 cups white flour and 1 cup wholemeal flour

**1 teaspoon bicarbonate of soda**

**1 teaspoon ground ginger**

**Currents for decorating**

### Method

1. Preheat oven to 160°C (325°F).

2. Prepare 2 large flat oven trays by spraying with cooking spray.

3. Cream butter margarine, sugar and vanilla.

4. Gradually add egg to creamed mixture, beating well after each addition.

5. Pour in golden syrup and beat well.

6. Sift white flour, bicarbonate of soda and ginger into creamed mixture and mix well. Stir in wholemeal flour. When substituting wholemeal flour, it may be necessary to add a little milk to sufficiently moisten dough. Dough should be a firm consistency.

7. Turn dough out onto a lightly floured board and knead lightly. Roll half the dough to 0.5 cm (¼ in) thickness.

8. Using a gingerbread cutter, cut out gingerbreads and carefully lift onto prepared trays.

9. Decorate as desired.

10. Place into a moderate oven and bake for approximately 15 minutes or until golden brown.

11. When cooked, remove from oven and leave on trays for 2 minutes. Loosen Gingerbreads and leave on trays to cool.

12. When completely cold, store in an airtight container.

# Jam Drops

Makes approximately 20 biscuits
Preparation time: 15 minutes
Cooking time: Convection cookery 15 minutes

## Ingredients

125g (4 oz) butter 90 g (3 oz) salt-reduced margarine
$^3/_4$ cup caster sugar $^1/_2$ cup caster sugar
$^1/_2$ teaspoon vanilla essence
2 eggs, 1 whole egg and 1 egg white lightly beaten
1$^3/_4$ cups white self-raising flour 1 cup white self-raising flour and
$^3/_4$ cup wholemeal self-raising flour
1 teaspoon baking powder
$^1/_4$ cup cornflour
$^1/_4$ cup custard powder
Jam (of your choice) use jam with no added sugar as desired

## Method

1. Preheat oven to 160°C (325°F).
2. Prepare 2 flat oven trays by spraying with cooking spray.
3. Cream butter margarine, sugar and vanilla.
4. Gradually add egg to creamed mixture, beating well after each addition.
5. Sift white flour, baking powder, cornflour and custard powder into creamed mixture and mix well. Stir in wholemeal flour. When substituting wholemeal flour, it may be necessary to add a little milk to sufficiently moisten mixture. Mixture should be a firm consistency.
6. Roll portions of mixture into balls approximately the size of a walnut and place onto prepared trays.
7. Make a 1 cm ($^1/_2$ in) hole in the centre of each biscuit with the handle of a wooden spoon dipped in flour.
8. Place $^1/_2$ teaspoon jam into the centre of each biscuit. Take care not to put too much jam into each biscuit, or it will run out during cooking.
9. Place into a moderately slow oven and bake for approximately 15 minutes or until golden brown.
10. When cooked, remove from oven and leave on trays for 2 minutes. Loosen biscuits and leave on trays to cool.
11. When completely cold, store in an airtight container.

# Jam Tarts

Make approximately 4 dozen tarts
Preparation time: 30 minutes
Cooking time: Convection cookery 12 minutes

## Ingredients

250 g (8 oz) butter 180 g (6 oz) salt-reduced mono-unsaturated margarine
185 g (6 oz) sugar 150 g (5 oz) sugar
$^1/_2$ teaspoon vanilla essence
1 egg, lightly beaten
375 g (13 oz) white flour 300 g (10$^1/_2$ oz) white flour and 75 g (2$^1/_2$ oz) wholemeal flour
$^1/_2$ teaspoon baking powder
60 g (2 oz) cornflour
60 g (2 oz) custard powder
Jam of your choice for tarts (approx. 1 x 300 ml jar raspberry jam) use jam with no added sugar as desired

## Method

1. Preheat oven to 190°C (375°F).
2. Prepare 4 patty trays by spraying with cooking spray.
3. Cream butter margarine, sugar and vanilla.
4. Gradually add egg to creamed mixture, beating well after each addition.
5. Sift white flour, baking powder, cornflour and custard powder into creamed mixture. Stir in wholemeal flour. Mix to a firm dough. When substituting wholemeal flour, it may be necessary to add a little milk to sufficiently moisten mixture. Mixture should be a firm consistency.
6. Turn out onto a lightly floured board and knead lightly. Roll out to 0.5 cm ($^1/_4$ in) thickness.
7. Cut 6.5 cm (2$^1/_2$ in) circles of pastry. Carefully lift circles of pastry into prepared trays.
8. Place 1 teaspoon of jam into each tart shell.
9. Roll out small portions of pastry and decorate tops of tarts.
10. Place into a moderately hot oven and bake for approximately 12 minutes or until pale golden brown.
11. When cooked, remove from oven and leave in trays for 6 minutes, before carefully lifting out onto a fine wire rack to cool.

Jam Tarts
(see recipe
opposite page)

## Macaroons

Makes approximately 24 Macaroons
Preparation time: 20 minutes
Cooking time: Convection cookery 50 minutes

### Ingredients

2 cups caster sugar 1½ cups caster sugar
2 egg whites
1 teaspoon white vinegar
2 tablespoons boiling water
2 teaspoons cornflour
½ teaspoon baking powder
¼ teaspoon vanilla essence
¾ cup coconut ½ cup coconut

### Method

1. Preheat oven to 200°C (400°F).
2. Prepare a flat baking tray by lining with baking paper.
3. Place caster sugar, egg whites, vinegar and boiling water into a large bowl. Beat until mixture is stiff enough to hold its own peaks. It is best to use a heavy-duty electric mixer for this process.
4. Sift cornflour and baking powder into bowl. Stir into egg white mixture.
5. Stir in vanilla and coconut.
6. To shape macaroons, use a large piping bag and a large star nozzle and pipe small portions onto prepared tray, or alternatively place tablespoons of mixture onto prepared tray.
7. Place into a moderately hot oven and immediately reduce heat to 150°C (300°F) for 20 minutes to dry out macaroons. Reduce heat to 100°C (225°F) for 30 minu, or until Macaroons are dried out.
8. When cold, remove from oven and leave on a tray for 6 minutes to cool.
9. Loosen Macaroons and leave on tray to cool
10. When completely cold, store in an airtight container.

## Melting Moments

This name has been given to this traditional way of making biscuits that will melt in the mouth for just a moment!

Makes approximately 20 biscuits
Preparation time: 12 minutes
Cooking time: Convection cookery 15 minutes

### Ingredients

200 g (7 oz) unsalted butter 150 g (5 oz) salt-reduced mono-unsaturated margarine
⅓ cup caster sugar ¼ cup caster sugar
½ teaspoon vanilla essence
2 cups white flour 1½ cups white flour and ½ cup wholemeal flour
½ cup cornflour

### Method

1. Preheat oven to 160°C (325°F).
2. Prepare a flat oven tray by spraying with cooking spray.
3. Cream butter margarine, sugar and vanilla.
4. Stir white flour and cornflour into creamed mixture and mix well. Stir in wholemeal flour. When substituting wholemeal flour, it may be necessary to add a little milk to sufficiently moisten mixture. Mixture should be a firm consistency.
5. Using a biscuit forcer, shape small portions onto prepared tray. Alternatively, using lightly floured hands, roll portions of mixture into balls approximately the size of a walnut and place onto prepared tray. Use a fork dipped in flour to press flat.
6. Place into a moderately slow oven and bake for approximately 12 minutes or until pale golden brown.
7. When cooked, remove from oven and leave on tray for 2 minutes. Loosen biscuits and leave on tray to cool.
8. When completely cold, store in an airtight container.

# Meringues

Makes approximately 20 Meringues
Preparation time: 20 minutes
Cooking time: Convection cookery 50 minutes

## Ingredients

2 cups caster sugar  1¹/₂ cups caster sugar

2 egg whites

1 teaspoon white vinegar

2 tablespoons boiling water

2 teaspoons cornflour

¹/₂ teaspoon baking powder

¹/₄ teaspoon vanilla essence

## Method

1. Preheat oven to 200°C (400°F).
2. Prepare a flat baking tray by lining with baking paper.
3. Place caster sugar, egg whites, vinegar and boiling water into a large bowl. Beat until mixture is stiff enough to hold its own peaks. It is best to use a heavy-duty electric mixer for this process.
4. Sift cornflour and baking powder into bowl. Stir into egg white mixture.
5. Stir in vanilla.
6. To shape meringues, use a piping bag and a large star nozzle and pipe small portions onto prepared tray, or alternatively place tablespoons of mixture onto prepared tray.
7. Place into a moderately hot oven and immediately reduce heat to 150°C (300°F) for 20 minutes to dry out meringues. Reduce heat to 100°C (225°F) for 30 minutes longer or until Meringues are dried out.
8. When cold, remove from oven and leave on tray for 6 minutes to cool.
9. Loosen Maeringues and leave on tray to cool
10. When completely cold, store in an airtight container.

# Orange Biscuits

Makes approximately 20 biscuits
Preparation time: 15 minutes
Cooking time: Convection cookery 15 minutes

## Ingredients

125g (4 oz) butter 90 g (3 oz) salt-reduced mono-unsaturated margarine

125g (4 oz) caster sugar 100 g (3¹/₂ oz) caster sugar

¹/₂ teaspoon vanilla essence

1 egg, lightly beaten

Finely grated rind 1 orange

1 cup desiccated coconut omit coconut and use ¹/₂ cup buckwheat kernels

1¹/₂ cups white self-raising flour, sifted 1¹/₂ cups wholemeal self-raising flour

## Method

1. Preheat oven to 160°C (325°F).
2. Prepare 2 flat oven trays by spraying with cooking spray.
3. Cream butter margarine, sugar and vanilla.
4. Gradually add egg to creamed mixture, beating well after each addition.
5. Stir in orange rind and coconut buckwheat kernels.
6. Sift white flour into creamed mixture and mix well. Stir in wholemeal flour. When substituting wholemeal flour, it may be necessary to add a little milk to sufficiently moisten mixture. Mixture should be a firm consistency.
7. Using lightly floured hands, roll portions of mixture into balls approximately the size of a walnut and place onto prepared trays. Use a fork dipped in flour to press flat.
8. Place into a moderately slow oven and bake for approximately 15 minutes or until golden brown.
9. When cooked, remove from oven and leave on trays for 2 minutes. Loosen biscuits and leave on trays to cool.
10. When completely cold, store in an airtight container.

# Pikelets

Makes approximately 25 pikelets depending on the size
Preparation time: 10 minutes
Cooking time: Convection cookery 20 minutes

## Ingredients

3 eggs 2 whole eggs and 1 egg white
1 cup caster sugar ³/₄ cup caster sugar
1 cup milk 1 cup low-fat milk
3 tablespoons butter 2 tablespoons salt-reduced mono-unsaturated margarine
¹/₄ teaspoon bicarbonate of soda
¹/₂ teaspoon vanilla essence
2 cups white self-raising flour 1 cup white self-raising flour and 1 cup wholemeal self-raising flour

## Method

1. Separate eggs.
2. Place egg whites into a large dry, clean mixing bowl. Beat whites until they hold stiff peaks.
3. Gradually add caster sugar to egg whites, beating well after each addition.
4. Place egg yolks into a small bowl and beat well.
5. Lightly beat egg yolks and gradually stir into egg white mixture. Lightly beat egg whites and gradually stir into egg white mixture.
6. Pour milk into a jug.
7. **Convection cookery**
   Place butter margarine into a small saucepan and melt over a gentle heat. or
   **Microwave cookery**
   Place butter margarine into a small microwave-safe bowl. Cover and microwave on high for 40 seconds or until butter margarine is melted.
8. Pour melted butter margarine into milk in jug. Stir in bicarbonate of soda and vanilla.
9. Sift white flour into a medium-sized mixing bowl. Stir in wholemeal flour.
10. Add flour and liquid alternately to the egg mixture, mixing well after each addition. When substituting wholemeal flour, it may be necessary to add a little more milk to sufficiently moisten mixture. Mixture should be a batter consistency.
11. Heat an electric frypan to 170°C (340°F). (Point no. 7 on a dial of 1-10.)
12. Spray pan with cooking spray.
13. Place tablespoons of mixture into pan.
14. Cook until bubbles appear on the surface. Turn and cook on reverse side until golden brown.
15. Place a tea towel over a fine wire rack. When cooked, remove pikelets from frypan and place onto tea towel. Cover to prevent drying out.

# Pumpkin Scones

Makes approximately 15 scones
Preparation time: 20 minutes
Cooking time: Convection cookery 12 minutes

## Ingredients

60 g (2 oz) butter 40 g (1¹/₂ oz) salt-reduced mono-unsaturated margarine
60 g (2 oz) caster sugar 40 g (1¹/₂ oz) caster sugar
¹/₂ teaspoon vanilla essence
1 egg, lightly beaten
1 cup cold, cooked mashed pumpkin
¹/₂ cup milk ¹/₂ cup low-fat milk
2¹/₂ cups white self-raising flour, ¹/₂ cup white self-raising flour, and 2 cups wholemeal self-raising flour
A little extra milk a little extra low-fat milk (for glazing)

## Method

1. Preheat oven to 200°C (400°F).
2. Prepare a flat oven tray by spraying with cooking spray.
3. Cream butter margarine, sugar and vanilla.
4. Gradually add egg to creamed mixture, beating well after each addition.
5. Mix in pumpkin.
6. Gradually add milk and stir well.
7. Sift white flour into mixture and mix well. Stir in wholemeal flour. When substituting wholemeal flour, it may be

Piklets (see recipe opposite page)

Damper (back) (see recipe page 17)
Pumpkin Scones (see recipe page 106)

8. Turn out onto a lightly floured board and knead lightly. Pat out to 2.5 cm (1 in) thickness.
9. Dip a 3 cm (1¼ in) cutter in flour. Cut out rounds and place onto prepared tray.
10. Glaze with a little extra milk.
11. Place into a hot oven and bake for approximately 12 minutes or until golden brown and cooked.
12. When cooked, remove from oven and leave on tray for 2 minutes. Place onto a fine wire rack to cool.

## Scones (Nanna's Scones)

Those children who have a Nanna who spends time teaching them to cook are very lucky. I would like to dedicate this recipe to my children's Nanna, who gave them so much pleasure by teaching them how to make scones. I trust that other Nannas who read this book will try this recipe and allow their grandchildren to help them make scones.

I have memories of my children having scone dough of all shapes and sizes in all areas of the kitchen benches. Children must learn, and it is only instruction and patience that will teach them.

Nanna made the lightest scones I have ever tasted and her secret to success is written here for you to experience as you make your perfect batch of scones.

Makes approximately 15 scones
Preparation time: 20 minutes
Cooking time: Convection cookery 12 minutes

Scones are best when made and eaten the same day. If you are not able to do this, it is possible to securely wrap scones and freeze them.

### Ingredients

**3 cups white self-raising flour.** 3 cups wholemeal self-raising flour
**3 tablespoons butter** 2 tablespoons salt-reduced mono-unsaturated margarine
**1½ cups milk** 1½ cups low-fat milk
**A little extra milk** a little extra low-fat milk **(for glazing)**

### Method

1. Preheat oven to 200°C (400°F).
2. Prepare a flat oven tray by spraying with cooking spray.
3. Sift white flour into a medium sized mixing bowl. Add wholemeal flour.
   Rub butter margarine into flour with the tips of the fingers until mixture resembles fine breadcrumbs. This process may be done using an electric food processor.

4. Make a well in the centre of the dry ingredients. Pour in milk. Use a knife to stir milk into dry ingredients. Stir from the centre to the outside and mix well. When substituting wholemeal flour, it may be necessary to add a little more milk to sufficiently moisten mixture. Mixture should be a firm consistency.
5. Turn out onto a lightly floured board and knead lightly. Pat out to 2.5 cm (1 in) thickness.
6. Dip a 3 cm (1¼ in) cutter in flour. Cut out rounds and place onto prepared tray.
7. Glaze with a little extra milk.
8. Place into a hot oven and bake for approximately 12 minutes or until golden brown and cooked.
9. When cooked, remove from oven and leave on tray for 2 minutes. Place onto a fine wire rack to cool.

## Shortbread

The festive season is the time to serve shortbread. Some people serve it at Christmas while others prefer to serve it at New Year.

Makes approximately 24 shortbread
Preparation time: 20 minutes
Cooking time: Convection cookery 12-15 minutes

### Ingredients
375 g (12 oz) unsalted butter 300 g (10 oz) unsalted butter or salt-reduced mono-unsaturated margarine
180 g (6 oz) soft icing sugar mixture (sifted) 150 g (5 oz) soft icing sugar mixture
½ teaspoon vanilla essence
1 tablespoon honey
500 g (1 lb) white flour 375 g (12 oz) white flour and 125 g (4 oz) wholemeal flour

### Method
1. Preheat oven to 150°C (300°F).
2. Use 6 cm (2¾ in) individual foil trays or spray patty pans with cooking spray.
3. Cream butter margarine, icing sugar, vanilla and honey.

4. Sift white flour into creamed mixture and mix well. Stir in wholemeal flour. When substituting wholemeal flour, it may be necessary to add a little milk to sufficiently moisten mixture. Mixture should be a firm consistency.
5. Using lightly floured hands, roll portions of mixture into balls approximately the size of a walnut and place into foil trays. Use a fork dipped in flour to press flat or decorate as desired.
6. Place into a moderately slow oven and bake for approximately 12-15 minutes or until very pale golden brown.
7. When cooked, remove from oven and leave in foil trays to cool.
8. When completely cold, store in an airtight container.

## Tart Shells

Makes approximately 30 tart shells
Preparation time: 20 minutes
Cooking time: Convection cookery 10 minutes
These tart shells can be baked ahead of time and stored in an airtight container until required.

### Ingredients
125 g (4 oz) butter 90 g (3 oz) salt-reduced mono-unsaturated margarine
½ cup caster sugar ⅓ cup caster sugar
½ teaspoon vanilla essence
1 egg, lightly beaten
180 g (6 oz) white flour 90 g (3 oz) white flour and 90 g (3 oz) wholemeal flour
½ teaspoon baking powder
30 g (1 oz) cornflour
30 g (1 oz) custard powder

**Method**

1. Preheat oven to 200°C (400°F).
2. Individual 6 cm (2¹/₂ in) foil trays are best for making these tarts.
3. Cream butter margarine, sugar and vanilla.
4. Gradually add egg to creamed mixture, beating well after each addition.
5. Sift white flour, baking powder, cornflour and custard powder into creamed mixture and mix well. Stir in wholemeal flour. When substituting wholemeal flour, it may be necessary to add a little milk to sufficiently moisten dough. Dough should be a firm consistency.
6. Turn dough out onto a lightly floured board and knead lightly. Divide dough in half. Roll half the dough to approximately 0.5 cm (¹/₄ in) thickness.
7. Using a 6.5 cm (2³/₄ in) fluted cutter, cut out rounds of pastry.
8. Carefully lift into individual foil trays.
9. Gently press pastry into each foil tray.
10. Place tart shells onto a flat oven tray.
11. Place into a moderately hot oven and bake for 5 minutes. Reduce heat to 180°C (350°F) and bake for a further 5 minutes or until pastry is lightly golden brown and firm to touch.
12. When cooked, remove from oven and leave on tray to cool.
13. When completely cold, store in an airtight container.

# Miscellaneous

## Beef Stock

Preparation time: 1¹/₂ hours
Cooking time: Convection cookery 2 hours
Microwave cookery 1 hour

## Ingredients

2 kg (4 lb) beef bones
2 teaspoons salt omit salt
Freshly ground black pepper (as desired)
3 litres (6 pt) cold water
I carrot, peeled and finely diced
I turnip, peeled and finely diced
I brown onion, peeled and finely diced
2 sticks celery, finely diced
Bouquet garni (selection of herbs and spices of your choice, tied in a piece of fine muslin)
12 peppercorns
12 whole cloves
2 bay leaves

## Method

1. Wash bones and chop, if necessary. Trim excess fat from bones.
2. Put bones into a large bowl. Add salt omit salt, pepper and water.
3. Allow to stand for 1 hour.
4. **Convection cookery**
   Place bones and liquid into a large saucepan. Bring slowly to the boil. Simmer with lid on for

1 hour. Add vegetables, bouquet garni, peppercorns, cloves and bay leaves. Simmer for a further 1 hour or until meat and vegetables are soft. or

**Microwave cookery**

Place bones and liquid into a large microwave-safe bowl. Microwave on high for 30 minutes and stir. Add vegetables, bouquet garni, peppercorns, cloves and bay leaves. Microwave for a further 30 minutes on medium-high or until meat and vegetables are soft.

5. Allow to cool.
6. Allow liquid to set and remove surface fat.
7. Strain and reserve liquid. Discard remainder.
8. Store stock in the refrigerator or freezer until required.

## Brandy Chocolates

Chocolates are what I term a 'sometimes' food. It is acceptable to have them occasionally.

Makes approximately 40 chocolates
Preparation time: 15 minutes

### Ingredients

60 g (2 oz) unsalted butter 30 g (1 oz) unsalted butter or salt-reduced monounsaturated margarine

1/2 cup pure icing sugar

1 teaspoon vanilla essence

1 tablespoon brandy (Other alcohol or flavours can be substituted for brandy.)

1 egg yolk

200 g (7 oz) dark cooking chocolate 180 g (6 oz) dark cooking chocolate

### Method

1. Prepare a large flat tray by covering with plastic wrap.
2. Cream butter margarine, icing sugar, vanilla and brandy.
3. Add egg yolk to creamed mixture and beat well.
4. **Convection cookery**
   Place chocolate into the top of a double saucepan. Melt chocolate over a low heat. or
   **Microwave cookery**

Place chocolate into a medium-sized microwave-safe bowl. Microwave on medium-high for 1 minute and stir. Continue to microwave on medium-low, stirring at 30-second intervals, until chocolate is melted.

5. Slowly pour melted chocolate into creamed mixture, beating constantly.
6. Allow mixture to firm a little if necessary before using.
7. Spoon mixture into a piping bag with a large star nozzle and pipe stars onto prepared tray. Alternatively, place tea-spoons of mixture onto prepared tray.
8. Place in refrigerator to set.
9. Store in a covered container in the refrigerator until required.

## Caramel (for Tart Shells)

This caramel is suitable as a filling for Tart Shells. See recipe for tart shells on page 109.

Preparation time: 20 minutes
Cooking time: Convection cookery 7-10 minutes
Microwave cookery 4-5 minutes

### Ingredients

1 tablespoon butter 1 teaspoon salt-reduced monounsaturated margarine

1 cup brown sugar 3/4 cup brown sugar

1 tablespoon cornflour

1 cup milk 1 cup low-fat milk

2 eggs, lightly beaten

1/2 cup thickened cream omit cream

1/2 teaspoon vanilla essence

### Method

**Convection cookery**

1. Place butter margarine into a small saucepan and melt over a gentle heat. Stir in sugar and mix well. Remove saucepan from heat.
2. Place cornflour into a medium-sized bowl. Blend with a lit-tle of the milk. Add remainder of milk and stir well.
3. Gradually add blended cornflour to melted butter

margarine and sugar in saucepan. Pour egg into saucepan and mix well. Return to heat and bring to the boil. Boil for 3 minutes stirring constantly until mixture thickens. Remove from heat.

4. Allow to cool before stirring in cream omit cream and vanilla. or

**Microwave cookery**

1. Place butter margarine into a medium-sized microwave-safe bowl. Microwave on high for 30 seconds.
2. Stir in sugar. Microwave on high for 1 minute and stir.
3. Place cornflour into a medium-sized bowl. Blend with a little of the milk. Add remainder of milk and stir well. Gradually add to melted butter margarine in bowl. Pour egg into bowl and mix well.
4. Microwave on high for 1 minute and stir. Continue to microwave on medium-high, stirring at 1 minute intervals until mixture thickens.
5. Allow to cool before stirring in cream omit cream and vanilla.

Store in an airtight container in the refrigerator. The reduced-sugar variety will not keep as long. When required, put caramel into tart shells just before serving.

# Caramel Sauce

Makes 2 x 300 ml (10 oz) jars
Preparation time: 10 minutes
Cooking time: Convection cookery 5 minutes
Microwave cookery 4 minutes

## Ingredients

**90 g (3 oz) unsalted butter** 60 g (2 oz) unsalted butter or salt-reduced mono-unsaturated margarine
**1 cup dark brown sugar** ³/₄ cup dark brown sugar
**1 cup warm water**
**2 tablespoons golden syrup**
**2 tablespoons cornflour**
**3 tablespoons cold water**
**¹/₄ cup whipped cream** omit cream and use ¹/₄ cup reduced-fat evaporated milk

## Method

1. **Convection cookery**

   Place butter margarine, sugar, warm water and golden syrup into a small saucepan. Bring to the boil. Reduce heat and cook for 2 minutes stirring constantly. Put cornflour into a separate small bowl. Blend with cold water. Stir into mixture in saucepan. Cook over a gentle heat until sauce thickens, stirring constantly. or

   **Microwave cookery**

   Place butter margarine, sugar, warm water and golden syrup into a small microwave-safe bowl. Microwave on high for 1 minute and stir. Continue to microwave on medium-high, stirring at 30-second intervals until butter margarine is melted. Put cornflour into a separate small bowl. Blend with cold water. Stir into mixture in bowl. Microwave on high for 1 minute and stir. Continue to microwave on medium-high, stirring at 30-second intervals until sauce thickens.
2. Allow to cool slightly. Stir in cream omit cream and stir in reduced-fat evaporated milk.
3. While still warm, bottle in warm sterilised jars and seal.
4. Store in the refrigerator until required.

# Chicken Stock

Preparation time: 1½ hours
Cooking time: Convection cookery 2 hours
Microwave cookery 1 hour

## Ingredients

1 x 3 kg (6 lb) chicken
2 teaspoons salt omit salt
Freshly ground black pepper (as desired)
3 litres (6 pt) cold water
1 carrot, peeled and finely diced
1 turnip, peeled and finely diced
1 brown onion, peeled and finely diced
2 sticks celery, finely diced
Bouquet garni (selection of herbs and spices of your choice, tied in
a piece of fine muslin)
12 peppercorns
12 whole cloves
2 bay leaves

## Method

1. Wash chicken and roughly chop. Trim fat from chicken.
2. Put chicken pieces into a large bowl. Add salt omit salt,
   pepper and water.
3. Allow to stand for 1 hour.
4. **Convection cookery**
   Place chicken and liquid into a large saucepan. Bring slowly
   to the boil. Simmer with lid on for
   1 hour. Add vegetables, bouquet garni, peppercorns, cloves
   and bay leaves. Simmer for a further 1 hour or until chicken
   and vegetables are soft. or
   **Microwave cookery**
   Place chicken and liquid into a large microwave-safe bowl.
   Microwave on high for 30 minutes and stir. Add vegetables,
   bouquet garni, peppercorns, cloves and bay leaves.
   Microwave for a further 30 minutes on medium-high or
   until chicken and vegetables are soft.
5. Allow to cool.
6. Allow liquid to set and remove surface fat.
7. Strain and reserve liquid. Discard remainder.
8. Store stock in the refrigerator or freezer until required.

# Chocolate Sauce

Makes 2 x 300 ml (10 oz) jars
Preparation time: 10 minutes
Cooking time: Convection cookery 5 minutes
Microwave cookery 4 minutes

## Ingredients

100 g (3 ½ oz) unsalted butter 60 g (2 oz) unsalted butter or
salt-reduced mono-unsaturated margarine
1 cup dark brown sugar ¾ cup dark brown sugar
1 cup warm water
2 tablespoons golden syrup 1 tablespoon golden syrup
2 tablespoons cornflour
3 tablespoons cocoa
3 tablespoons cold water
¼ cup whipped cream omit cream and use ¼ cup reduced-fat
evaporated milk

## Method

1. **Convection cookery**
   Place butter margarine, sugar, warm water and golden syrup
   into a small saucepan. Bring to the boil. Reduce heat and
   cook for 2 minutes, stirring constantly. Put cornflour and
   cocoa into a separate small bowl. Blend with cold water.
   Stir into mixture in saucepan. Cook over a gentle heat until
   sauce thickens, stirring constantly. or
   **Microwave cookery**
   Place butter margarine, sugar, warm water and golden syrup
   into a small microwave-safe bowl. Microwave on high for
   1 minute and stir. Continue to microwave on medium-
   high, stirring at 30-second intervals until butter margarine
   is melted. Put cornflour and cocoa into a separate small
   bowl. Blend with cold water. Stir into mixture in bowl.
   Microwave on high for 1 minute and stir. Continue to
   microwave on medium-high, stirring at 30-second intervals
   until sauce thickens.
2. Allow to cool slightly. Stir in cream omit cream and stir in
   reduced-fat evaporated milk.
3. While still warm, bottle in warm sterilised jars and seal.
4. Store in the refrigerator until required.

## Coffee Cream

This delicious coffee cream can be served with coffee or with icecream as desired.

Makes 2 x 300 ml (10 fl oz) bottles
Preparation time: 10 minutes

### Ingredients

1 x 415 g (14 oz) can condensed milk 1 x 415 g (14 oz) can lite condensed milk

1 ¹/₂ cups good quality whisky

3 tablespoons Chocolate Sauce (see recipe page 113)

2 teaspoons instant coffee

2 eggs 1 egg

300 ml (9 fl oz) cream omit cream and use 300 ml (9 fl oz) reduced-fat evaporated milk

¹/₂ teaspoon vanilla essence

### Method

1. Place all the ingredients together in the bowl of an electric blender. Blend well.
2. Bottle and seal.
3. Store in the refrigerator until required.

## Marmalade

Marmalade is usually a popular spread for breakfast toast. This recipe includes 4 citrus fruits to make a very flavoursome marmalade.

Makes approximately 5 x 300 ml (10 oz) jars
Preparation time: 30 minutes (to cut up fruit)
Cooking time: Convection cookery 1 hour
Microwave cookery 30 minutes

### Ingredients

4 oranges

2 lemons

1 grapefruit

1 lime

7 cups boiling water

8 cups sugar 6 cups sugar

### Method

1. Finely slice fruit and retain seeds. Place fruit into a large bowl. Pour in 6 cups boiling water. Seal bowl and leave overnight. Place seeds into a small bowl. Pour remaining 1 cup boiling water over seeds. Seal bowl and leave overnight.
2. **Convection cookery**
   Next day place fruit and water into a large saucepan. Strain liquid from seeds. Add liquid to saucepan. Tie seeds in a small piece of fine muslin. Add to contents of saucepan. Bring to the boil and reduce heat. Simmer with the lid on until peel is soft. Gradually add sugar and stir until sugar is dissolved. Boil with lid off until jam gels when tested on a cold saucer. Stir occasionally to prevent fruit sticking to bottom of saucepan. Remove from heat. Discard seeds. or
   **Microwave cookery**
   Next day place fruit and water into a large microwave-safe bowl. Strain liquid from seeds. Add liquid to saucepan. Tie seeds in a small piece of fine muslin. Add to contents of bowl. Cover with vented plastic wrap. Microwave on high for 5 minutes and stir. Continue to microwave at 4-minute intervals and stir until mixture boils and peel is soft. Add half the sugar and stir. Microwave on high for 3 minutes. Stir in remainder of sugar. Microwave on high for 3 minutes and stir. Continue to microwave at 4 minute intervals and stir until jam gels when tested on a cold saucer. Discard seeds.
3. While still warm, bottle in warm sterilised jars and seal.

The reduced sugar variety will not keep as long and should be stored in the refrigerato.

Marmalade (see recipe opposite page)

# Lemon Spread (for Tart Shells)

This is very popular as a spread for bread or filling for Tart Shells. It can be prepared quickly by using a food processor and cooking in the microwave oven. See recipe on page 109 for Tart Shells.

Makes 3 x 300 ml (10 oz) jars
Preparation time: 7 minutes
Cooking time: Convection cookery 7 minutes
Microwave cookery 5 minutes

## Ingredients

**4 eggs** use 3 whole eggs and 1 egg white
1½ cups caster sugar 1 cup caster sugar
1 tablespoon cornflour
¼ cup water
Finely grated rind 1 lemon
1 cup lemon juice (made from approx. 4 lemons)
125 g (4 oz) unsalted butter 90 g (3 oz) unsalted butter or salt-reduced mono-unsaturated margarine

## Method

1. Place all the ingredients except butter margarine into an electric food processor. Blend until ingredients are well combined.
2. **Convection cookery**
   Pour blended ingredients into a medium-sized saucepan. Add butter margarine. Stir constantly over a gentle heat until mixture thickens, taking care not to boil or the mixture may curdle. or
   **Microwave cookery**
   Pour blended ingredients into a medium-sized microwave-safe bowl. Add butter margarine. Microwave on high for 1 minute and stir. Continue to microwave on medium-high, stirring at 1 minute intervals until mixture thickens.
3. While still warm, bottle in warm sterilised jars and seal.

Lemon Spread is best stored in the refrigerator. The reduced-sugar variety will not keep as long.

# Taco Sauce

This is a very tasty sauce that can be stored in the refrigerator where it will keep for 1 week. It can be used for tacos and pizzas, for flavouring casseroles or it can be served as an accompaniment with meals. It has no added fat.

Makes approximately 2 x 300 ml (10 oz) jars
Preparation time: 15 minutes
Cooking time: Convection cookery 7 minutes
Microwave cookery 5 minutes (approximately)

## Ingredients

2 tomatoes
Boiling water
1 clove garlic, peeled and crushed
1 small onion, peeled and cut into small dice
½ teaspoon hot paprika
2 tablespoons tomato paste 2 tablespoons no added salt tomato paste
3 tablespoons sugar 2 tablespoons sugar
3 tablespoons herb or white vinegar
½ teaspoon pepper sauce
1 tablespoon cornflour

## Method

1. Place tomatoes into a small bowl. Cover with boiling water and leave for 2 minutes. Remove skins. Roughly chop tomatoes.
2. Blend all the ingredients in the bowl of an electric food processor or blender.
3. **Convection cookery**
   Pour mixture into a small saucepan. Stir over a gentle heat until mixture boils and thickens. or
   **Microwave cookery**
   Pour mixture into a small microwave-safe bowl. Microwave on high for 2 minutes and stir. Continue to microwave on high, stirring at 1 minute intervals, until sauce boils and thickens.
4. While still warm, bottle in warm sterilised jars and seal. Refrigerate until required.
   Sauce will keep in the refrigerator for approximately 1 week.

# White Sauce

This basic white sauce can be used to pour over vegetables or used as required.

Preparation time: 6 minutes
Cooking time: Convection cookery 7 minutes
Microwave cookery 4 minutes (approximately)

## Ingredients

2 tablespoons butter 1 tablespoon salt-reduced mono-unsaturated margarine or 1 tablespoon olive oil
2 tablespoons white flour 1 tablespoon cornflour and 1 tablespoon wholemeal flour
300 ml ($\frac{1}{2}$ pt) milk 300 ml ($\frac{1}{2}$ pt) low-fat milk
Salt omit salt
$\frac{1}{4}$ teaspoon pepper (as desired)

## Method

1. **Convection cookery**
   Place butter margarine or oil into a small saucepan. Heat over a gentle heat. Remove saucepan from heat. Stir in white flour cornflour and wholemeal flour. Return to heat and cook over a gentle heat for
   1 minute, stirring constantly. Remove from heat. Gradually stir in milk. Return to heat and cook over a gentle heat, stirring constantly, until mixture boils and thickens. Season with salt omit salt and pepper. or
   **Microwave cookery**
   Place butter margarine or oil into a small microwave-safe bowl. Cover and microwave on high for 30 seconds or until butter margarine is melted. Stir in flour. Stir in cornflour and wholemeal flour. Microwave on high for 40 seconds and stir. Gradually stir in milk. Microwave on high for 1 minute and stir. Continue to microwave, stirring at 1 minute intervals until mixture boils and thickens. Season with salt omit salt and pepper.

# Yorkshire Pudding

Yorkshire pudding is a traditional accompaniment to roast beef (see recipe page #). The best way to cook it is to roast the beef on a trivet and place the pudding batter in the juices under the meat. The juices drip onto the pudding giving a delicious flavour. If cooking spray is used instead of dripping when roasting the beef, the fat content will be reduced as only the juice from the meat will collect in the bottom of the baking dish during cooking.

To make a light batter, thorough beating is required. The beating introduces cold air into the mixture; on heating in the oven, the air expands and lifts or lightens the batter. If the batter is made correctly, it is not necessary to add any other raising agent. Some people prefer to add a little baking powder to the mixture.

Preparation time: 1 hour 10 minutes
Cooking time: Convection cookery 20-30 minutes

## Ingredients

1 cup white flour $\frac{1}{2}$ cup white flour and $\frac{1}{2}$ cup wholemeal flour
Salt (as desired) omit salt
$\frac{1}{4}$ teaspoon baking powder (as desired)
1 egg, lightly beaten
1$\frac{1}{4}$ cups milk 1$\frac{1}{4}$ cups low-fat milk
Use baking dish juices from cooking Roast Beef for cooking Yorkshire pudding or use $\frac{1}{2}$ cup dripping $\frac{1}{2}$ cup olive oil

## Method

1. Sift white flour, salt omit salt and baking powder if used into a small mixing bowl. Stir in wholemeal flour.
2. Make a well in the centre of the flour. Add egg.
3. Stir in flour from the sides of the bowl, adding half the milk a little at a time. When half the milk is used, all the flour must be moistened.
4. Beat well. It is essential to remove lumps and incorporate air into the mixture to make a light batter.
5. When batter is smooth, add remaining milk. A whisk may be used to mix in remaining milk.

6. Allow to stand for 1 hour. This is essential to allow the gluten to develop in the moistened dough.

7. Preheat oven to 200°C (400°F).

8. Heat dripping olive oil in a baking dish. If using meat juices in a baking dish in which Roast Beef was cooked, this also will need to be heated. (If you are going to cook Yorkshire Pudding under beef that is already cooking, you won't need to preheat oven or melt dripping. Place Yorkshire Pudding into juices in baking dish, $\frac{1}{2}$ hour before meat is cooked.)

9. Pour batter into heated dripping olive oil or baking dish juices. Place baking dish into oven and bake for approximately 20 to 30 minutes.

10. Cut into triangles or squares for serving.